Vertamae Cooks Again

More Recipes from The Americas' Family Kitchen℠

Vertamae Cooks Again

More Recipes from The Americas' Family Kitchen℠

Vertamae Grosvenor
Companion to the public television series

Food photography by Geoffrey Nilsen
Design by David Albertson Design, SF

BAY BOOKS

San Francisco

This book is dedicated to all those who have cooked for me, and to those I have cooked for: here's to the good times, the good table talk, and the good food.

This book is published to accompany the second season of the series *The Americas' Family Kitchen.*" This series is a production of the Chicago Production Center at WTTW and More Than Equal Productions, Ltd.

Bay Books is an imprint of Bay Books & Tapes, Inc., 555 De Haro St., No. 220, San Francisco, CA 94107.

Editor: Carolyn Miller
Art Direction and Design: David Albertson Design, SF
Copy Editor: Ken Della Penta
Food Photographer: Geoffrey Nilsen
Food Stylist: Susan Massey
Cover portrait: Heimo
Additional text by Carolyn Miller
Proofreader: Virginia Simpson-Magruder
Indexer: Ken Della Penta
Photos: p.v B. Bachman/American Stock; p.ix Dr. Andrec/American Stock; p.xiv and p.22 K. Rice/American Stock; p.31 K. Carpenter/American Stock; p.38 H. L. Bunker/American Stock; p.50 R. Krubner/American Stock; p.68 and p.155 Douglas Adesko; p.89 C. Seghers/American Stock; p.121 V. Clevenger/American Stock; p.126 Blumebild/American Stock

The publishers wish to thank Graycliff, the five-star restaurant and hotel in Nassau, Bahamas, for permission to reprint recipes on pages 11, 36, and 106 from the book *Graycliff The Legend* © 1992. Special thanks to the Garzaroli family and head chef Ashwood Darville.

Every reasonable effort has been made to obtain permission from the copyright holders of previously published materials. Navajo Fry Bread (p.64), from *I Hear America Cooking* by Betty Fussell © 1986 Betty Fussell, is used by permission of Viking Penguin, a division of Penguin Putnam Inc.; Callalou (p.18), Buttermilk Biscuits (p.59), and Codfish and Ackee (p.110) are reprinted from *Vibration Cooking* by Vertamae Grosvenor by permission of Ballantine Books, a division of Random House, Inc.; Black Cake (p.134), from *Soul and Spice: African Cooking in the Americas* by Heidi Haughy Cusick © 1986, is used by permission of Chronicle Books.

Library of Congress Cataloging–in–Publication Data:
Smart-Grosvenor, Vertamae
    Vertamae Cooks Again : More Recipes from The Americas' Family Kitchen /
  Vertamae Grosvenor ; food photography by Geoffrey Nilsen.
      p.   cm.
    "Companion to the public television series."
    ISBN 0-912333-91-X (pbk. : alk. paper)
    1. Afro–American cookery. 2. Cookery, Caribbean. 3. Cookery, Latin American. 4. Cookery, African. 5. Americas' family kitchen (Television program) I. Americas' family kitchen (Television program) II. Title.
TX715.S6368   1999
641.59'29601812--dc21   99-21127
                                                                  CIP

ISBN 0-912333-91-X

Printed in China
10 9 8 7 6 5 4 3 2 1

Distributed by Publishers Group West

Zora Neale Hurston wrote, "I was born with the map of Dixie on my tongue." Well, I was born with a taste of Dixie on mine. You may have the taste of Oaxaca, Ontario, or Cuba on yours. At the risk of sounding like one of those parents who think theirs are the cutest, smartest children, I say that if home is the Americas, home tastes good!

—Vertamae Grosvenor

Contents

Entrées 69

Desserts and Beverages 127

Introduction

Nothing can take you home faster than the fragrance and the sight of food from home. In his poem "The Tropics in New York," Jamaican-born poet Claude McKay longed for a taste of home when he saw coconuts, mangoes, and other tropical foods on a cold day in that northern city.

Bananas ripe and green, and ginger-root,
Cocoa in pods and alligator pears
And tangerines and mangos and grape fruit
Fit for the highest prize at parish fairs,

Set in the window, bringing memories
Of fruit-trees laden by low-singing rills,
And dewy dawns, and mystical blue skies
In benediction over nun-like hills.

My eyes grew dim, and I could no more gaze;
A wave of longing through my body swept,
And, hungry for the old, familiar ways,
I turned aside and bowed my head and wept.

The Mende people of Sierra Leone have a phrase: "The language you cry in." You can grow up, leave your home, travel far, change your walk, your talk, your name, but you—your people, your roots—will always be known by the language you cry in. That's the language of home. And, like Claude McKay, I think that the natural truth is: That home language is about food, too.

I was born and raised in Hampton and Allendale County, South Carolina—the Low Country. That's home to me, and whether I was listening to the fish stories of my father and his friends or shelling peas on the porch with Grandmama Sula and my aunties, home taught me about food and love, and the love of food.

I come from a family where everybody cooked—men, women, and children. I still rememeber the day I cooked my very first pot of perfect rice—where every grain is dry and separate—and my Grandmama Sula asked, "Who cooked this rice?" Oh, man, I felt like my heart would burst—I did! I mean, I felt wonderful. Because for Geechee/Gullah people like mine, perfect rice is...well, perfect.

There are some who say you can't go home again: I say bah, humbug to that! Sometimes you just have to. Sometimes that craving for a taste of home comes down so hard you just have to have it—whatever "it" is. For me...through the lens of memory I can see Grandmama Sula "jarring up the summer": making watermelon rind preserves, canning tomatoes, beans, and other vegetables and fruits. Grandmama Sula made the most wonderful biscuits in the world, and with her fig preserves and freshly churned butter, they are a taste of home I have a permanent longing for.

In my grown-up life, I've become a traveling woman—like a lot of people in the Americas. So I speak from experience about that longing, that feeling so strong in your soul you just have to yield to it and start home-cooking no matter where you are. I can't speak bad about the food of any place I've been, but when that home hunger hits me, I will find me a stove and cook my own food. I've fixed my hoppin' John on New Year's Day in Paris, fried chicken in Johannesburg, and cooked salmon cakes and grits in Malibu.

What I find, as I travel, is that it's pretty much the same for everyone: If you are from someplace (and isn't everyone?), you take that place with you when you leave, or find it where you go, or maybe a little of both. Food

It's amazing the way people love to talk about their foods and how they "fix" them! And when they find out that you are curious about their home foods, that's when they really talk! And if you get really, really lucky, they might actually invite you into the kitchen.

is the absolute, bar none, best of all ways to take it (because the taste memories are so strong), find it (because foods may change their names, but they travel, too), or make it. And this is what I love about the language of food: I can make it for myself and feel at home, or share who I am with other people.

While I long for the taste of home, I don't miss the tough conditions: a water pump outside, an icebox and a woodburning stove inside. I look back in wonder on those kitchen days. How did Grandmama Sula and all of the others stand the heat in the kitchen, and how did they turn out those perfect breads, cakes and pies, pots of "proper," every-grain-to-itself rice, and kettles of steaming soups and stews?

The conditions might have been hard, but the experiences and memories have served me well. I've been traveling what I call the Afro-Atlantic foodways for nearly thirty years; for this new book and series, I sampled the broader North American foodways. In all these travels, I've usually found myself up to the challenge of different kitchens.

It's amazing the way people love to talk about their foods and how they "fix" them! And when they find out that you are curious about their home foods, that's when they really talk! And if you get really, really lucky, they might actually invite you into the kitchen. I have been lucky this way on more than one occasion. I've been able to meet people and become friends so that whenever and wherever we are together, we cook home—theirs and mine.

I'll tell you a story about my passion for other peoples' home cooking. In the '60s, I was living with my family on the Lower East Side of Manhattan. Talk about a lot of people far from home and bound and determined to bring it with them! On one block, you could get Greek, you could get deli, you could go to the Polish butcher or the kosher butcher—you could get almost any kind of food. To live in a city like that is a remarkable privilege.

One of my neighbors on Avenue A was a Sicilian woman named Carlotta. Carlotta was a great cook, and she cooked something different every day, because her husband Joe didn't like leftovers. She was always giving me bowls of food—I got to try the leftovers. We were both curious cooks, and we got into "How did you fix that?" and "How did you make this?" We became such good kitchen buddies that soon I was making ziti and she was making "proper" rice.

That curiosity about other people's home foods was always there for me, but this was the first kitchen that was mine, where I decided what to cook. So one day, I got the idea, why not take a country a month and only cook dishes from that country? So I did. For a whole month, I would cook breakfast, lunch, and dinner from the cuisine of one country—Greece or Spain, Mexico or Russia: I did them all.

For me, this exploration was nothing but fun. I was traveling, and never leaving the city! I also learned about some preferences and talents of my own. I was excellent in Greece, where, I was surprised and happy to learn, they eat a lot of okra. I was fabulous in Italy (I think Carlotta's influence helped). I was very good in China; I had a head start on the rice. France?

Well...all those sauces: After you get the thing done, you have to dunk it and drown it. It was not my favorite way to go about things, and it showed. I'll tell you what inspired me most: the Scandinavian food. You see, I would be nowhere without hot peppers. I mean, I literally have to have them (my cousin Betty once said to me, "I hope you stay healthy, because if a doctor ever tells you you can't have hot pepper, I'm afraid you'll die."). So when I cooked my way around the world back on Avenue A, I had to make up my own riffs on everything Scandinavian, adding hot pepper. To me, this sort of "fusion cooking" is terrific, and it's so often possible in the Americas, with this amazing shifting set of people.

My kids had a different take on the great experiment, being the guinea pigs—they hated it. Well, they hated it when I messed up. My daughter also hated going shopping. I would send her to this Italian store ten blocks away to get Arborio rice for risotto. She was not crazy about going so far, to a store full of unfamiliar food (while she walked, she used to practice pronouncing what she had to ask for) to get something that, as far as she was concerned, could be found right around the corner. But what she learned was that this is the rice I needed for this particular dish; and she and her sister also learned (like me, if not as willingly) that sometimes you can explore the world in your own neighborhood. These days, my childrens' children are unbelievably knowledgeable about food: When they are hungry they'll say things like, "Oh, I don't feel like having pizza, I want a pupusa!"—which is, incidentally, a heavenly thing from El Salvador: a cornmeal pancake stuffed with cheese, meat, or beans. I love

to imagine what they will pass on to their kids.

Of course, "ethnic" markets and restaurants don't exist just for strangers to get a taste of a different culture. They have to stay honest for the folks who come in for that taste of home. And if it tastes like home the folks will come. I witnessed that in New York; every day they'd travel to Atlantic Avenue in Brooklyn for the proper seasoning for their couscous and callaloos. On Saturdays, the suits, male and female, come home from the 'burbs to the market on 116th Street and Park Avenue for fresh-killed guinea hens; and on Sundays the cars pull away from Katz's on Houston Street, full of knishes, lox, and other deli delights.

There are two kinds of discoveries you make in "ethnic" markets and restaurants. One thing is, you start wondering, "What is it that people make with that?" And you start asking people, and if you do your asking with real curiosity and respect, they will tell you. Something interesting happens, and you learn—it's a true cultural exchange. Another thing you discover is how a plateful of home is a comfort to just about everyone.

There are other kinds of discoveries I've made, too, in my travels. I've been to tiny villages and big cities all around the Americas and other places in the world. One experience I've had firsthand, over and over again, is that Afro-Atlantic foodways are strong and deep throughout the African diaspora. Foods and ways with food may change their names and addresses a hundred times, but still keep to the same language people learned to cry in, if you know what I'm saying.

I've lifted the lid on many a pot in many a place and found a taste of home—my home—in there. In Brazil, miles away from Grandmama Sula's kitchen, I saw a field of collard greens on the way from the airport outside Bahia. Later that night I ate some of those greens along with okra and a rice dish with a strange name, but clearly a cousin to what we call a perlou in South Carolina. In a funky café in the Bahamas, I ate a black-eyed pea soup: The dumplings were new but the peas were very familiar. In Haiti, what they called yams sure tasted like sweet potatoes to me. In Mexico, the fried grasshoppers and other insects were a first, but the hospitality was of the classic Southern kind I grew up with.

Recently, with the new television series (and here, in its companion book), I've been looking at North American foodways in a larger sense and discovering that the culinary crossing of cultures and cooking styles brings interesting changes to kitchens all over the Americas. The television crew and I sampled home foods from Mexico to Canada and a lot of places in between—Haiti and the Bahamas, to name a couple—and we found a lot of the old and familiar in with the new. Everywhere in the hemisphere there are people cooking with what's already there and making it theirs. Grits and shrimp belong to Charleston the same way boiled fish and grits belong to Nassau. And aren't tortillas corn bread? I've found that food that has traveled far can be the homiest food of all—whether we call it rice and peas or hoppin' John, paella or perlou, corn meal mush, cou cou, or polenta.

You could say this ability to adapt is the gift of all our presence—the presence of those who were already here and those who came to the so-called New World. Out of necessity—out of our circumstances and the needs of our bodies and souls for home food—came a freedom to find new ways of cooking and eating and being at home. I'll end with a story. In 1989, the president of Sierra Leone visited the South Carolina Low Country. Scholars had uncovered the many cultural connections between his country and the region, once the home of great rice plantations. The European planters didn't know how to grow the rice, so they bought slaves from what was called "the rice coast" in West Africa—part of which is now the coast of Sierra Leone. The enslaved Africans were skilled in the cultivation of rice, and the planters became some of the wealthiest men in the colony.

In honor of the President's visit, the tables groaned with rice dishes. Red rice. Peas and rice. Shrimp and rice. Chicken and rice. Okra and rice. Beans and rice. Oysters and rice. Eggplant and rice. Lots of greens—and I'm not talking about salad greens; I mean collards and kale. And lots of hot pepper. Now, I was sitting nearby, and I saw the President after he finished eating several plates lean back in his chair and say, "It tastes just like home."

Acknowledgments

My sincere appreciation to all those at WTTW who worked so hard in *The Americas' Family Kitchen,*^{SM} especially the interns and the back-kitchen cooks.

Very special thanks to editors Clancy Drake and Carolyn Miller for their expertise and patience.

Thanks to Connie Shorter and Sidney Jackson, who still greet me with a smile in spite of a few smoky times when I was testing the recipes.

Thanks to Dudley, Martha, Maria, and Guadeloupe for a taste of home in Mexico. Thanks to Alex, Ernest, and Monique for the flavors of Haiti.

Thanks to WABE's Milton Clipper and Delores Campbell for keeping *The Americas' Family Kitchen*^{SM} in Atlanta's face. Ditto to Abena Joan Brown and Val Grey Ward for doing the same thing in Chicago.

Thanks to my lawyer, Amy Goldson, my agent, Marie Dutton Brown, and Sistuh Margaret Porter Troupe, the best biscuit maker from Mississippi to California.

For their continual support, encouragement, and sense of humor, I thank my family. Special thanks and hugs to "the rich sweet pastries" (they know who they are).

Soups

Calvin's Black-Eyed Pea Soup with Dumplings

2 cups dried black-eyed peas

1 tablespoon olive oil

1 onion, chopped

1 stalk celery, chopped

1 small green bell pepper, seeded, deribbed, and chopped

3 cloves garlic, minced

1 bay leaf

1 teaspoon dried thyme, crumbled

1 ham hock, or 4 ounces thick-sliced bacon or salt pork, chopped

1 cup coconut milk

Salt and freshly ground black pepper to taste

Cayenne pepper to taste

Leaves from 1 sprig thyme, minced

1 (12-ounce) package potato gnocchi

Serves 6

This is my adaptation of a memorably mouthwatering soup I tasted two decades ago in Nassau, when my dear friend, master carpenter, fabulous actor, and grand chef Calvin Lockhart took me to a small beachside joint. Now, coming from Carolina I thought I knew a thing or two about black-eyed peas, but when I had them as a soup and with dumplings, too—yummy yummy yum! When I tasted that soup, as Gullah people say, I shut my mouth wide open.

My interpretation of the soup includes coconut milk, and because I find dumplings to be sometimey—sometimes they come out right, and sometimes they don't—I use Italian dumplings, or gnocchi. They don't act up. Actually, gnocchi are quite appropriate for this soup, as Calvin spent years in Italy and his Italian is flawless.

Pick over and rinse the peas. Soak the peas overnight in cold water to cover by 2 inches. Drain and place in a stockpot with cold water to cover by 2 inches.

In a skillet over medium heat, heat the oil and sauté the onion, celery, bell pepper, and garlic for about 5 minutes. Add the onion mixture, bay leaf, and dried thyme to the peas and bring to a boil. Skim off any foam that rises. Add the ham hock, bacon, or salt pork. Reduce the heat to low, cover the pot, and simmer until the peas are tender, about 1$1/2$ hours.

Remove 1$1/2$ cups of peas from the pot. In a blender or food processor, combine the 1$1/2$ cups peas and the coconut milk and purée until smooth. Return the purée to the pan. Add the salt, black pepper, cayenne pepper, fresh thyme, and gnocchi. Bring to a simmer and cook for 15 minutes, or until the gnocchi are tender and heated through. Adjust the seasonings. Remove and discard the bay leaf. Take the meat off the ham hock, if using, and return it to the soup.

EVERY CULTURE HAS ITS "GOOD LUCK" charms. In the South, it's black-eyed peas. If you haven't had at least one helping of black-eyed peas on New Year's Day for good luck, you are courting disaster for the coming year.

Kidney Bean Soup

2 cups dried kidney beans

2¹/₂ quarts water or chicken broth

4 ounces salt pork

1 stalk celery, chopped

1 cup chopped scallions

2 sprigs thyme

2 sprigs parsley

2 bay leaves

Freshly ground pepper to taste

Minced Scotch bonnet chili to taste

Salt to taste

Serves 6

This soup is quite popular in Haiti. It's a family standby because you can serve it thick, over rice, or you can add more liquid when more folks show up for dinner. Any bean, including black-eyed peas, can be used to make this soup. You can also purée only part of the beans for a different texture.

Pick over and rinse the beans. Soak the beans overnight in water to cover by 2 inches. Drain the beans and place in a large saucepan. Add all but 1 cup of the water or broth. Add all the salt pork, celery, scallions, thyme, parsley, bay leaves, pepper, and chili. Bring to a boil, reduce the heat to low, cover, and cook until tender, about 2¹/₂ hours. Remove the salt pork and bay leaves and add salt. Purée the soup in batches in a blender. Return to the saucepan. Heat the remaining 1 cup water or stock and add to the soup. Stir to blend. Taste and adjust the seasonings and serve.

THE SCOTCH BONNET, SAID TO BE THE hottest of all chilies, is the chili of choice in the Caribbean. Its appearance is distinctive. Small, round, yellow, and pleated, it is named after the traditional Scottish tam-o'-shanter, which it resembles. Take care with this one: wear rubber gloves when handling it, and add less than the recipe calls for if you don't like hot food.

Calde Verde

(Kale Soup)

2 tablespoons olive oil

1 pound linguiça, kielbasa, or
   other garlicky sausage,
   sliced

1 large onion, chopped

5 boiling potatoes, peeled and
   chopped

6 cups water

3 or 4 cups thinly sliced kale or
   collard greens

   Salt and freshly ground black
   pepper to taste

   Cayenne pepper to taste
   (optional)

Serves 4 to 6

This hardy Cape Verdean soup is wonderful. Sometimes I make it with collards. Sometimes I make it with kale. But I always eat it with corn bread. It's a comfort soup, like an old friend. Which reminds me of the old Cape Verdean proverb: "There is no better mirror than an old friend."

In a skillet over medium heat, heat 1 tablespoon of the olive oil and sauté the sausage and onion until lightly browned, about 8 minutes. Set aside. In a stockpot, combine the potatoes and water, bring to a boil, and cook the potatoes until tender, about 20 minutes. Mash them in the water with a potato masher. Add the greens to the pot and simmer for 10 minutes. Add the sausage mixture and the remaining 1 tablespoon olive oil. Simmer for 5 minutes. Add salt, black pepper, and cayenne, if using.

Three Sisters Soup

2 tablespoons corn oil
1 onion, sliced
2 cloves garlic, crushed
2 small zucchini or yellow
    crookneck squash, sliced
4 scallions, chopped
2 tablespoons chopped fresh
    cilantro
1 tablespoon dried oregano,
    crumbled
1 tablespoon dried thyme,
    crumbled
1 tablespoon yellow cornmeal
2 cups corn kernels
1 (10-ounce) package frozen
    lima beans
3 cups vegetable broth or
    chicken broth
    Salt and freshly ground pepper
    to taste
    Minced fresh basil, for garnish

Serves 4 to 6

In traditional Native American cooking, vegetables, beans, and grains are key ingredients that show up in dishes throughout the Americas. Corn, squash, and beans were so important to the Native American diet that they were known as the three sisters, so this soup is called Three Sisters Soup.

In a stockpot over medium heat, heat the oil and sauté the onion and garlic until translucent, about 4 minutes. Add the zucchini, scallions, cilantro, oregano, thyme, cornmeal, corn, and lima beans. Sauté for about 3 minutes. Add the broth and salt and pepper and bring to a boil, then reduce the heat to a simmer. Cover and cook for about 45 minutes, stirring occasionally. Sprinkle with the basil and serve.

THERE ARE TWO BASIC KINDS OF SQUASH, winter and summer. Winter squash can be kept in its gourd, or shell, for quite a while after harvesting. Summer squash must be eaten within a short time. Squash is as American as pumpkin pie! The pumpkin is just one of the many different kinds of squash that have been in the Americas for a very long time—so long, in fact, that archeologists have found evidence of squash being grown in Mexico at least seven thousand years ago. Only fifty years after Columbus landed in the Caribbean, squash from the Americas was being distributed all across Europe, and the Europeans came up with their own names for it, like zucchini.

Iroquois Maize Soup

3 cups chicken broth

2 tablespoons yellow cornmeal

2 tablespoons minced cilantro

2 cloves garlic, crushed

2 tablespoons chopped fresh
  basil

1 onion, sliced

1/2 teaspoon freshly ground
  pepper

1 1/2 cups fresh or frozen corn
  kernels

  Pinch of salt

1 (10-ounce) package frozen lima
  beans

8 ounces flounder fillets

Serves 4 to 6

You know, we really don't stop to think about it all that much, but many of the foods we enjoy today and some of our most popular cooking methods were developed thousands of years ago by Native Americans. Before the Europeans arrived in the New World, the land was cultivated with amazing creativity. Native peoples honored the land with spirituality. And they adapted to it with remarkable ingenuity. Corn was the most important of all the foods grown by the Native Americans, whose word for this grain was *mahiz,* or maize.

In a stockpot, bring the broth to a simmer. Stir in the cornmeal, cilantro, garlic, basil, onion, pepper, corn, and salt and cook for 10 minutes. Add the lima beans and simmer for 15 minutes more, stirring occasionally. Break the flounder into bite-sized pieces and add to the pot. Reduce the heat to low and cook for 10 minutes. Serve hot.

ONE OF THE CROPS DEVELOPED BY THE Incas was a special bean that grew faster than other beans in the mountains and took less time to cook. After the Incas were conquered by the Spanish and forced to abandon their capital city of Cuzco, this special bean was given the name of the new capital city of Peru: Lima. Of course, today the lima bean is popular throughout the U.S. South, where it is called the butter bean.

Carolina Minestrone

2   tablespoons olive oil
1   onion, diced
3   cloves garlic, minced
2   stalks celery, diced
1/2 green bell pepper, seeded,
      deribbed, and chopped
2   carrots, diced
3   tomatoes, chopped
2   boiling potatoes, peeled and
      chopped
2   zucchini, chopped
1   handful green beans, snapped
      small
5   cups vegetable broth or
      chicken broth
1/2 teaspoon dried oregano,
      crumbled
1/2 teaspoon dried thyme,
      crumbled
    Salt and freshly ground black
      pepper to taste
    Cayenne pepper to taste
1/4 cup long-grain white rice
1/2 cup chopped fresh parsley
1/2 cup chopped fresh cilantro
    Lemon or lime wedges, for
      serving
    Minced serrano chilies, for
      serving

Serves 6

Usually minestrone has pasta, but this one has rice instead. I call this Carolina Minestrone because of the rice. We Carolinians eat rice like Italians eat pasta. In Italian, minestrone means "big soup," and this is a big nutritious and delicious soup with lots of vegetables. I like it with crusty corn bread.

In a stockpot over medium heat, heat the olive oil and sauté the onion and garlic for 2 or 3 minutes. Add all the other vegetables and sauté for about 5 minutes. Add the broth and bring to a boil. Add the oregano, thyme, salt, black pepper, and cayenne pepper. Reduce the heat to a simmer and cook for 30 minutes. Add the rice and cook for another 30 minutes, or until the rice is tender. Taste and adjust the seasonings. Stir in the parsley and cilantro. Serve with lemon or lime wedges and serrano chilies.

EARLY IN THE SEVENTEENTH CENTURY, the British tried and failed to grow rice in Virginia. But thanks to African slaves and the marshes of the Low Country, rice grew so well in South Carolina that it became known as "Carolina gold." To this day, rice is the essential ingredient of Low Country cuisine.

Crema Poblana

2 tablespoons unsalted butter

1/4 onion, finely chopped

1 clove garlic, minced

2 cups milk

1 cup chicken broth

1/2 tablespoon cornstarch

1/2 cup heavy cream

1 sprig epazote (optional)

1 poblano chili, roasted, seeded, deribbed, and finely sliced

1/2 cup fresh or frozen corn kernels

1/2 teaspoon salt

Freshly ground white pepper to taste

1/4 cup crumbled queso fresco or feta cheese, for garnish

2 tablespoons minced fresh cilantro or flat-leaf parsley, for garnish

Serves 4

You will *love* this soup! It's adapted from a recipe by Dudley Nieto, a Mexican chef and native of Puebla, where they have their own special kind of cuisine, including the poblano chili and mole poblano (*poblano* means it's from Puebla, also the home of beautiful tiles). This is a delicate, comforting soup. You know it's good because it has corn, cream, poblano chili, and cheese in it.

In a saucepan, melt the butter over low heat. Add the onion and garlic and cook until translucent, about 3 minutes. Whisk in the milk and broth. In a small bowl, whisk the cornstarch and cream together. Bring the soup to a simmer and whisk in the cornstarch mixture. Add the epazote (if using), the chili, corn, salt, and pepper. Simmer, uncovered, for about 15 minutes. Taste and adjust the seasonings. Serve in shallow soup bowls, garnished with the cheese and the cilantro or parsley.

Grouper Soup with Puff Pastry

1 pound grouper, red snapper, or
    sea bass fillets, diced
  Juice of 1 lemon or lime
  Salt to taste
4 slices bacon, diced
2 small potatoes, peeled and
    diced
1 stalk celery, diced
1 onion, diced
4 cups water
1 Scotch bonnet chili, minced
2 tablespoons crushed pepper-
    corns
2 sheets defrosted frozen puff
    pastry
1 egg, beaten with 1 tablespoon
    water

  Serves 4

Grouper soup is a traditional Bahamian dish, so much so that
the classic recipe is called "fish tea" (see the recipe on page 14).
Graycliff, the five-star restaurant in Nassau, has a more sophisticated, Frenchified version, topped with circles of puff pastry.

Sprinkle the diced fish with lemon or lime juice and salt. Divide
among four 6-inch soufflé dishes.

In a skillet over medium heat, cook the bacon until the fat is rendered. Add the potatoes, cover, and cook for about 5 minutes. Add
the celery and onion, cover, and cook for another 5 minutes. Add the
water and bring to a boil. Reduce the heat to low and add the chili
and salt to taste. Cover and cook until the vegetables are tender,
about 10 minutes.

Preheat the oven to 350°. Divide the soup among the dishes. Add the
crushed peppercorns. Cut the puff pastry into four 6-inch rounds.
Place a round on top of each serving of soup. Brush each round with
the egg mixture. Place the dishes on a baking sheet and bake for
about 10 minutes, or until the puff pastry is golden and puffed.
Serve hot.

*THERE ARE SEVERAL VARIETIES OF
groupers, a kind of sea bass, found on
both the Atlantic and Pacific coasts.*

*Any firm, white-fleshed fish can be
substituted for Bahamian grouper.*

Shrimp Soup

1 pound medium shrimp in the
  shell
6 cups water
2 fish heads (optional)
2 stalks celery, chopped
4 sprigs parsley
2 bay leaves
2 tablespoons olive oil
1 large onion, chopped
3 cloves garlic, minced
2 tomatoes, peeled and chopped
2 green plantains, peeled and
  sliced
3 boiling potatoes, peeled and
  cut into eighths
2 small sweet potatoes, peeled
  and chopped
3 tablespoons manioc flour (cassava meal or tapioca flour)
  Pinch of ground sage
1 cup fish broth, clam juice, or
  chicken broth
1 tablespoon minced fresh
  parsley

Serves 8 to 10

Here is a wonderful shrimp soup from the Cape Verde Islands, off the west coast of Africa. A lot of the Cape Verdean foods go back to the first island residents, who were Portuguese sailors and African slaves taken from the country of Guinea, in West Africa. In the nineteenth century, whalers from New England, who hunted in the area, stopped on the islands for supplies and to rest and hire sailors.

Today, the great-great-grandchildren of those sailors from Cape Verde are part of the Cape Verdean–American communities in Boston, New Bedford, and other New England towns, where traditional Cape Verdean dishes are still eaten. The manioc flour helps to thicken the soup; it is the same thing as tapioca flour. If you can't find it, use regular flour or cornstarch.

Shell the shrimp and reserve the shells. Place the shells in a stockpot with the water, the fish heads (if using), half the celery, the parsley sprigs, and 1 of the bay leaves. Bring to a boil, reduce the heat to a simmer, and cook for about 30 minutes. Drain the stock and return it to the pot.

In a stockpot over medium heat, heat the olive oil and sauté the onion, garlic, and tomatoes for about 5 minutes. Add the onion mixture, remaining celery, plantains, boiling potatoes, sweet potatoes, manioc flour, sage, and the remaining bay leaf to the shrimp stock and bring to a boil. Reduce the heat to a simmer and cook until the vegetables are tender, 15 to 20 minutes. Add the fish broth. Add the shrimp and cook just until pink, about 5 minutes. Taste and adjust the seasonings. Remove and discard the bay leaves. Sprinkle with the minced parsley and serve.

LIKE SOUTHERN COOKS, CAPE VERDEAN cooks have what we call the "hand," meaning each person's seasoning is different. So use these recipes as a guide. Make the dish your own—use your hand.

Be brave and expand your culinary horizons. Like the Cape Verdean proverb says, "Without leaving, there is no coming back."

Island Fish Tea

1 (1- to 2¹/2-pound) grouper, red
    snapper, or sea bass, cut into
    large pieces
2 fish heads
2 cloves, crushed
¹/4 cup chopped fresh chives
1 tablespoon chopped fresh
    parsley
6 allspice berries, crushed
6 black peppercorns, crushed
4 sprigs thyme
1 bay leaf
1 stalk celery, chopped
1 small onion, chopped
1 Scotch bonnet chili
    Salt to taste
    Juice of 2 limes

Serves 4 to 6

The cuisine of the Bahamas is built around their one abundant resource: seafood. There are so many delicious possibilities—grilled, fried, baked. And boiled fish is a specialty of the islands, served for breakfast with grits, a favorite in the southern parts of the United States. Grouper is probably one of the most popular fish on the Bahamian table, for breakfast, lunch, or dinner. Here is a soup made from grouper that the islanders call "fish tea."

Place the fish in a stockpot and add water to cover. Add the fish heads, cloves, chives, parsley, allspice, peppercorns, half the thyme, and the bay leaf. Bring to a boil, reduce the heat to a simmer, cover, and cook for 20 minutes. Drain the fish, reserving the liquid. Skin and bone the fish. Return the liquid and fish meat to the pot. Add the remaining thyme, the celery, the onion, and chili. Bring to a simmer, cover, and cook for 10 to 15 minutes. Add the salt and lime juice. Remove and discard the chili and bay leaf and serve.

BAHAMIAN CUISINE IS AN EXCITING reflection of the diversity of its people and is constantly evolving. "Fish tea" is one of the traditional recipes, but food writers have noted that a number of new chefs are taking a fresh look at the cuisine, adding a dash of new excitement to old favorites. Blending tradition with nouvelle cuisine. Taking risks. Being adventurous. After all, adventure is what the Bahamas are all about.

Nova Scotia Scallop and Potato Chowder

2 tablespoons olive oil

1 onion, finely diced

2 cloves garlic, minced

1/2 green bell pepper, seeded, deribbed, and diced

1 pound boiling potatoes, peeled and cubed

1/4 teaspoon ground saffron

2 tomatoes, chopped

4 cups fish broth, clam juice, or chicken broth

2 tablespoons unsalted butter

Salt and freshly ground pepper to taste

1 pound sea scallops

2 tablespoons chopped fresh parsley

Serves 6

Some people like making a dish one way and some like making it another, like chowders. New England clam chowder is white, and Manhattan clam chowder is red. Tomato makes the difference. This chowder from Nova Scotia also uses tomatoes.

In a stockpot over medium heat, heat the oil. Add the onion, garlic, and bell pepper and sauté for 5 minutes. Add the potatoes, saffron, and tomatoes; then stir in the broth. Add the butter, salt, and pepper. Bring to a boil, reduce the heat to low, and simmer for 20 minutes, or until the potatoes are tender. Add the scallops and cook for 5 minutes, or until they are opaque throughout. Taste and adjust the seasonings. Sprinkle with parsley and serve

NOVA SCOTIANS ARE SO PROUD OF their scallops and all the bounty of the land and sea that in 1989 they created the annual Taste of Nova Scotia festival. This island also has historical significance for African Americans. Two hundred years ago, the British promised freedom to blacks who fought for England during the American Revolutionary War. The British lost the war, but kept their promise. Over three thousand black British loyalists came to call Nova Scotia home.

Deer Scallop Chowder

1 thick slice bacon, finely
  chopped
1 onion, chopped
2 cloves garlic, minced
6 black peppercorns, cracked
1¹/₂ cups clam juice or fish broth
3 potatoes, peeled and diced
1 cup half-and-half
¹/₂ cup heavy cream
1 pound bay scallops
  Salt, and freshly ground black
  pepper to taste
  Cayenne pepper to taste
2 tablespoons unsalted butter
  Chopped fresh chives, for
  garnish

Serves 4 to 6

In Nova Scotia in the mid-1800s, there was an inn called Deer's Castle in the village of Preston. Deer's Castle was described as "a little weather-beaten shanty of boards that clung like flakes to the framework." The owner of the inn was a black man named William Deer, who thought very highly of his establishment and of his wife. An inscription on the swing sign in front of the inn read, "William Deer who lives here, keeps the best wine and beer, brandy cider and other good cheer, fish and ducks and moose and deer, caught and shot in the woods near, with cutlets or steaks as will appear, if you stop you need not fear. But you will be well treated by William Deer and by Mrs. Deer, his dearest deary dear."

A great percentage of Canada's scallops are shipped from Nova Scotia. Mr. Deer could very well have served this recipe at his inn, so I call it Deer Scallop Chowder.

In a heavy cast-iron pot, cook the bacon for 3 to 5 minutes over medium heat. Add the onion, garlic, and peppercorns. Add the clam juice and potatoes. Simmer until the potatoes are tender, about 15 minutes. Add the half-and-half and cream. Cook a few minutes to heat, then add the scallops. Simmer for 5 minutes, or until the scallops are opaque throughout. Be careful not to let the chowder boil. Add the salt, black pepper, and cayenne pepper. Swirl in the butter, sprinkle with chives, and serve.

WHEN MRS. DEER, WHO HAD BEEN A slave in Maryland, was asked to compare Nova Scotia and Maryland, she spoke of the harsh winters and the hard work it took to run the inn, but she said she liked Nova Scotia better. "In Maryland," she said, "I worked for other people; here I work for myself."

Callalou

2 tablespoons olive oil

1 large onion, finely chopped

4 cloves garlic, minced

8 ounces salt pork, chopped

1 pound ham hocks

3 quarts water

3 pounds callalou, collard
greens, or spinach, washed,
stemmed, and chopped

12 pods okra

1 Scotch bonnet chili, minced

1 teaspoon dried thyme,
crumbled

1 1/2 pounds fish fillets, skinned,
boned, and chopped

6 ounces fresh lump crabmeat,
picked over for shell

1/4 cup minced fresh flat-leaf
parsley

1/2 cup coconut milk
Salt and freshly ground white
pepper to taste

Serves 12

This is a variation on a recipe from my book *Vibration Cooking,* where it's called "Kalalou Noisy le Sec," named after a place in Paris where I lived for a while with my friend Arrone. Callalou is the West Indian version of Southern greens, and when you cook greens with fish, crabmeat, coconut milk, and Scotch bonnet chili, you have got yourself a really wonderful pot of food.

In a stockpot over medium-low heat, heat the oil and cook the onion and garlic until translucent. Add the salt pork, ham hocks, and water and bring to a boil. Reduce the heat to a simmer, cover, and cook for about 15 minutes.

Add the greens, okra, chili, and thyme and cook for about 15 minutes. Stir in the fish, crabmeat, parsley, and coconut milk. Cook for about 5 minutes, or until the fish is opaque throughout. Season with salt and pepper.

CALLALOU GREENS ARE THE LEAVES OF the taro root, a starchy tuber found all over the West Indies. You can buy canned callalou, but you really need fresh greens for this dish. Look for them in Caribbean markets, or just use collard greens or spinach.

Sopa de Albondigas
(Meatball Soup)

2¹/₂ quarts chicken broth

Meatballs

  8 ounces ground pork
  8 ounces ground beef
¹/₂ onion, chopped
  1 clove garlic, minced
¹/₂ teaspoon dried Mexican
     oregano
  1 tablespoon chopped fresh
     cilantro, plus more for
     garnish
  1 tablespoon chopped fresh mint
  1 egg, slightly beaten
  1 teaspoon ground cumin
     Salt and freshly ground pepper
     to taste

     Chopped canned green chilies
     or minced jalapeño, for
     garnish
     Lime wedges, for serving

     Serves 6 to 8

Mexicans love soup, or *"sopa,"* as my granddaughter Charlotte says. I don't speak Spanish, and she does. Once she asked me for some *"sopa"* and I thought she wanted to eat soap. Needless to say, that was and is a big grandmother joke! Charlotte loves this soup, so I also call it Charlotte's Sopa.

In a stockpot, bring the broth to a simmer.

To make the meatballs, combine the meat, onion, garlic, oregano, the 1 tablespoon cilantro, the mint, egg, cumin, salt, and pepper in a bowl. Mix together well with your hands. Form into bite-sized meatballs. Gently place the meatballs in the stock. Reduce the heat to low and simmer until the meatballs are cooked through, about 45 minutes.

Ladle the meatballs into bowls and cover with stock. Sprinkle with chopped cilantro and chopped green chilies or minced jalapeño. Serve with lime wedges on the side.

XALAPA—OR JALAPA—THE CAPITAL CITY of the state of Veracruz, is also the jalapeño capital of the world —which is fitting, since this hot little chili takes its name from the city.

Sopa de Elote a la Mixteca
(Corn Soup)

8 ounces poblano chilies

2 tomatoes, chopped

1/2 cup chopped onion

1 clove garlic

1 teaspoon canola oil

6 cups chicken broth

2 cups fresh or frozen corn
   kernels

2 zucchini, finely diced

2 sprigs epazote or cilantro

8 ounces Swiss chard, cut into
   fine shreds

   Salt and freshly ground pepper
   to taste

   Crumbled queso fresco or feta
   cheese, for serving

Serves 6

Here's another wonderful and filling Mexican *sopa,* or soup. Chef Dudley Nieto, a native of Puebla, Mexico, has a *sopa* that's a perfect meal starter or luncheon main course. This corn soup is from the Mixtec Indians in the state of Veracruz.

Over an open flame of a stove burner, or under a preheated boiler, roast the chilies, turning as necessary, until blackened on all sides. Place in a paper bag, close the bag, and let the chilies steam for 15 minutes. Peel off the skins; then seed and stem the chilies, and cut into fine strips. Set aside.

Using a blender, purée the tomatoes, onion, and garlic until smooth. In a saucepan over medium heat, heat the oil and sauté the tomato mixture for 5 minutes. Place the chicken broth in a large saucepan and bring to a simmer. Add the corn kernels and bring to a boil; then reduce the heat to low and simmer for 10 minutes. Add the zucchini, epazote, chilies, and Swiss chard. Add the tomato mixture and season with salt and pepper. Ladle the soup into bowls. Sprinkle with cheese and serve.

Salads

Afro-Mexican Radish Salad

4 cups cooked black beans

7 red radishes, thinly sliced

1/2 cup chopped fresh cilantro

8 ounces panela or feta cheese, crumbled

2 tablespoons freshly squeezed lemon juice

1/4 cup red wine vinegar

3/4 cup olive oil

Salt and freshly ground pepper to taste

Leaves from 2 heads lettuce optional

Serves 6

Ever since I found out about it, I've longed to be in Oaxaca on the Night of the Radishes, in December, just before Christmas. That's when people make elaborate displays of religious and historical scenes carved out of giant radishes. Prizes are given for the best displays. In honor of that event, here's my Afro-Mexican salad, made with black beans and radishes.

Combine the beans, radishes, and cilantro in a bowl. Toss. Add the cheese and toss again. In a small bowl, whisk the lemon juice, vinegar, and olive oil together. Season with salt and pepper. Add to the salad and toss once again. Serve over lettuce leaves, if desired.

Bow Tie Salmon Salad

8 ounces bow tie pasta

2 tablespoons olive oil

1 (14-ounce) can red sockeye
    salmon, drained and flaked

2 stalks celery, chopped

1 onion, chopped

1 tablespoon Dijon mustard

1 or 2 tablespoons sweet pickle
    relish

1 1/2 cups cooked green peas

Juice of 1/2 lemon

Salt and freshly ground pepper
    to taste

1/4 cup chopped fresh parsley

1/4 cup chopped fresh cilantro

Serves 4 to 6

Pasta salad is always a good traveler. Everybody knows the old macaroni and tuna salad, which I personally find to be a weary traveler. This bow tie salmon salad is an upscale cousin. Yes, sockeye is more expensive than tuna, but it's sooooo good. This salad is a portable feast. Take it any time you need to bring something. Trust me. Wherever you take a pan of this, you will get a great welcome. As Shakespeare wrote in *A Comedy of Errors,* "Small cheer and great welcome makes a merry feast!"

In a large pot of salted boiling water, cook the pasta until tender but still a little chewy, about 10 minutes. Drain and toss with the olive oil. In a large bowl, combine the pasta with all the remaining ingredients except the parsley and cilantro. Taste and adjust the seasonings. Cover and refrigerate for at least 3 or 4 hours or as long as overnight. Bring to room temperature. Toss with the parsley and cilantro when ready to serve.

Conch Salad

12 ounces fresh or defrosted
    frozen conch meat

1/4 cup diced red onion

1/2 stalk celery, chopped

1/2 green bell pepper, seeded,
    deribbed, and diced

1 clove garlic, minced
    Salt and freshly ground black
    pepper to taste
    Cayenne pepper to taste
    Minced Scotch bonnet chili to
    taste
    Juice of 1 lemon
    Juice of 1 lime
    Olive oil to taste

1 large tomato, diced (optional)
    Lettuce leaves, for serving

Serves 4 to 6

Fresh conch may be hard to find, though you can look for it in Chinese and Caribbean markets. But frozen conch is found in many fish markets and of course in Caribbean communities. (Conch is available canned, but the taste is oceans away from fresh.) To prepare conch, you can pound it or, as some do, cook it in a pressure cooker. I don't mess with pressure cookers, so I pound it.

Place the conch in a heavy plastic bag and pound with a mallet until it thins out. Chop the conch into small dice or shreds by hand or in a blender or food processor. In a large bowl, combine the conch, onion, celery, bell pepper, garlic, salt, black pepper, cayenne pepper, and chili. Add the lemon and lime juice. Mix well and add the olive oil. Mix well again. Cover and marinate in the refrigerator for 3 or 4 hours. Taste and adjust the seasonings. Add the tomato, if using. Spoon the salad on lettuce leaves and serve.

HERE'S A CONCH STORY FOR YOU. IT'S about my great-great-great-granddaddy, who was named Mott. He was seven feet tall, and they said he could jump so high that he could click his heels three times before he hit the ground. But most of all, he had a voice so powerful that on his plantation, they didn't need to use a conch shell to announce when it was quitting time. When he called out, "Quittin' time!", they heard him on plantations in the next county! This is a true story.

Saffron Rice Salad with Multicolored Peppers

Saffron Rice

1 1/2 cups chicken broth

1/2 teaspoon ground saffron

3/4 cup long-grain white rice

    Salt and freshly ground pepper
      to taste

2 tablespoons red wine vinegar

1 tablespoon freshly squeezed
    lemon juice

    Salt and freshly ground pepper
      to taste

1/4 cup olive oil

1/4 cup each diced red, orange,
    yellow, and green bell
    peppers

2 scallions, finely chopped,
    including green portions

2 tablespoons chopped cilantro,
    plus cilantro sprigs for
    garnish

2 tablespoons chopped fresh
    flat-leaf parsley

    Lettuce leaves, for serving

1 cup cherry tomatoes, halved

    Flat-leaf parsley sprigs, for
    garnish

Serves 4 to 6

We have wonderful peppers throughout the Americas, and this dish has red, orange, yellow, and green peppers in it. The saffron turns the rice yellow, so this rice salad is not only a crowd pleaser, but pretty.

To make the saffron rice: In a saucepan, bring the broth to a boil. Add the saffron and stir to dissolve. Stir in the rice, salt, and pepper. Reduce the heat to low, cover, and cook for 20 minutes. Let sit covered for about 5 minutes, then uncover and fluff with a fork.

In a large bowl, whisk the vinegar, lemon juice, salt, pepper, and oil together. Taste and adjust the seasonings. Remove and reserve 1 tablespoon of the dressing. Add the rice, bell peppers, scallions, cilantro, and chopped parsley to the dressing in the large bowl. Toss gently and serve on lettuce leaves. Surround the salad with the cherry tomatoes. Sprinkle the tomatoes with the reserved dressing. Garnish the salad with the herb sprigs.

PEPPERS ARE NOT ONLY PRETTY, THEY'RE great for seasoning. The Spanish who came to the Americas were excited by the variety of peppers they found— peppers in all sizes, colors, and tastes, from mild to hot. And to this day they are used throughout the Americas in sauces, stews, salads, and soups.

Jicama-Nopalitos Ensalada

1 large jicama, peeled and cut into julienne

Leaves from 1/2 head romaine lettuce, coarsely chopped

1/2 red onion, finely sliced

1 large güero chili, seeded and sliced (optional)

1 large nopal (cactus paddle), cleaned, roasted, and cut into julienne (see note, below)

1 mango, peeled, cut from the pit, and diced

Vinaigrette

1/4 cup freshly squeezed orange juice

1/4 cup pineapple juice

1/4 cup olive oil

2 tablespoons honey

Kosher salt and freshly ground black pepper to taste

Leaves from 1/2 head romaine lettuce

Cilantro sprigs, for garnish

Cayenne pepper to taste

Serves 4

This recipe, slightly adapted from one by Mexican chef Dudley Nieto, uses *nopalitos,* slices of a paddle from the prickly pear cactus. Look for the paddles fresh in Latino markets. The taste reminds me a little of avocados and artichokes, and it makes a really refreshing salad, especially with crunchy, crispy jicama. You can buy canned *nopalitos* if you must, but the fresh ones are much better.

In a salad bowl, combine the jicama, lettuce, onion, chili (if using), nopal pieces, and mango. Whisk all the vinaigrette ingredients together and gently toss with the ingredients in the salad bowl. Serve on a bed of romaine lettuce leaves, garnished with cilantro and sprinkled very lightly with cayenne pepper.

MAKING NOPALITOS: MAKE SURE YOU ARE wearing gloves, then cut off the edges and ends of the paddle and scrape off the little spines and bumps with a large knife. Lightly oil and salt the paddle, then roast it on a grill over a low fire or under a preheated broiler about 6 inches from the heat source, turning once or twice, until it is completely limp. Let cool to the touch, then cut into thin slices.

Thanks to the indigenous peoples of Mexico and Central America, the cuisines of the world are rich with such foods as corn, beans, squash, tomatoes, jicama, chocolate, avocados, papayas, guavas, vanilla, chilies, and many spices.

Chicken Salad with Grapes

2¹/2 cups cubed cooked chicken
1 stalk celery, diced
¹/2 cup mayonnaise
2 to 3 tablespoons diced red
   onion
1 tablespoon freshly squeezed
   lemon juice
   Salt and freshly ground white
   pepper to taste
1 cup seedless grapes
¹/4 cup slivered almonds
   Lettuce leaves, for serving

Serves 4 to 6

Many special occasions are celebrated outdoors. All kinds of reunions, like the Annual Mississippi Picnic held in Central Park in New York. Although I'm not from Mississippi, I went to the first one nineteen years ago. The paper said you didn't have to be from Mississippi to go, and that you should bring a skillet. I found out that that was just some Northern reporter cracking on Southerners. I believed it, and I was the only person there with a skillet, but the food was great. They had chicken fixed every way you can fix it. Here's one of my favorite ways, a chicken salad that you can take to any picnic. (But remember to keep it cold.)

Combine the chicken and celery in a bowl. In another bowl, combine the mayonnaise, onion, lemon juice, salt, and pepper. Mix well. Add to the chicken and toss. Add the grapes and almonds and toss. Taste and adjust the seasonings. Refrigerate for 1 or 2 hours. Serve on lettuce leaves.

For, lo, the winter is past, the rain is over and gone;
The flowers appear on the earth, the time of singing
*   of birds is come, and the voice of the turtle is*
*   heard on our land;*
The fig tree putteth forth her green figs, and the vines
*   with the tender grape give a good smell. Arise, my*
*   love, my fair one, and come away.*
—Song of Solomon, 2:11–13

Christians and Moors Salad

2 cloves garlic, minced

1/4 teaspoon salt, plus salt to
    taste

2 tablespoons red wine vinegar

2 tablespoons freshly squeezed
    lemon juice

1/2 cup olive oil, plus more for
    sprinkling

3 tablespoons chopped cilantro

2 1/2 cups cooked long-grain white
    rice

1 1/2 cups cooked black beans
    Freshly ground pepper to taste

3 tomatoes, diced
    Mixed romaine and watercress
    leaves, for serving
    Sliced avocado and tomato, for
    serving

Serves 6

You may be familiar with the hot dish Christians and Moors. The name of this dish tells us that it was originally Spanish, and that its ingredients are black beans and white rice. Now it's been adopted by the Cubans, and I've adapted it to a salad made from the same basic ingredients.

In a large bowl, using the back of a wooden spoon or a pestle, crush the garlic and the 1/4 teaspoon salt together. Whisk in the vinegar, lemon juice, the 1/2 cup olive oil, and half the cilantro. Add the rice and beans and toss gently. Add the pepper and toss. Taste and adjust the seasonings. Gently stir in the diced tomatoes and the remaining cilantro. Let the flavors marry for at least 1 hour at room temperature.

Serve over a bed of the greens, surrounded by avocado and tomato slices. Sprinkle the avocado and tomato with a little olive oil and salt and pepper.

Haitian Slaw

1/2 cup water

1 1/2 cups distilled white vinegar
    Salt to taste
    Pinch of sugar

4 cups shredded cabbage

3 carrots, shredded

2 onions, thinly sliced

4 cloves garlic, minced

1 to 3 Scotch bonnet chilies,
    minced

Serves 4 to 6

This slaw will last for days in the refrigerator. It's one of those dishes that you can just keep around. Just keep adding more vegetables to the bowl.

In a large bowl, whisk together the water, vinegar, salt, and sugar. Stir in all the remaining ingredients. Taste and adjust the seasonings. Mix well, cover, and refrigerate overnight, stirring occasionally.

It's the hot pepper that makes this slaw. If you don't like hot food, use the smallest amount of Scotch bonnet chili, supposedly one of the hottest of all the chilies. This is the perfect dish to serve with rice and beans. I even know someone who claims to make a sandwich with it.

Holiday Ginger Salad

3 oranges

1/4 cup water

2 tablespoons sugar

1/2 teaspoon grated fresh ginger

1/2 cup dried figs, sliced

2 apples, cored and sliced

1 banana, peeled and sliced

2 tablespoons freshly squeezed
lemon juice

1/2 cup dates, pitted and sliced

Lettuce leaves, for serving

1/2 cup flaked coconut

Serves 8

On Christmas in Barbados, June Mourillon and her family always went to midnight Mass at St. Joseph's Episcopalian Church. After church, the family would meet at her mother's house to have this delicious salad with eggnog.

Using a large knife, cut the top and bottom off the oranges down to the flesh. Place each orange on end and cut off the peel down to the flesh. Then, holding the oranges one at a time over a small, heavy saucepan, cut on either side of each membrane to release the orange segments. Squeeze the membranes over the pan to release the juice. Add the water, sugar, and ginger to the juice and bring to a boil. Reduce the heat to low and simmer for a few minutes until slightly thickened. Add the figs and set aside to cool.

In a bowl, combine the apples and banana. Sprinkle with the lemon juice and toss. Add the orange segments, dates, and figs. Toss with the syrup, cover, and refrigerate for 1 or 2 hours. Line a serving bowl with lettuce leaves. Add the salad and sprinkle with coconut.

A SPANISH PRIEST IS CREDITED WITH bringing the first banana root stocks to the Caribbean. This now-familiar fruit had a variety of different names until the Africans gave it the name banana.

Grilled Tuna and Vegetable Salad

4 (6-ounce) tuna fillets

8 radicchio leaves

8 tomato slices

1 *each* red and green bell pepper, seeded, deribbed, and
cut into 1-inch-wide strips

Olive oil, for coating

Salt to taste

Juice of 1/2 lemon

4 tablespoons unsalted butter,
melted

10 fresh basil leaves, chopped

Serves 4

A fine salad from Graycliff, the five-star restaurant in Nassau in
the Bahamas. You can make this in summer when you have the grill
set up, but you can also make it using a grill pan or a broiler. The
tuna and *all* the vegetables are grilled, making this a quick and elegant main-course salad.

Light a fire in a charcoal grill or preheat a gas grill or a broiler. Coat
the tuna, radicchio, tomato, and bell peppers with olive oil. Sprinkle
the tuna with salt.

Grill or broil the radicchio, tomato, and bell peppers for about 2 minutes on each side. Transfer the radicchio to the center of 4 plates and
top with the tomato. Place the bell pepper around the radicchio. Set
aside and keep warm.

Grill the tuna for about 2 minutes on each side for medium rare.
Place the tuna on top of the tomato slices. Whisk the lemon juice into
the melted butter and sprinkle each tuna fillet lightly with the lemon
butter sauce. Garnish with the chopped basil and serve.

*GRAYCLIFF BECAME NASSAU'S FIRST INN
in 1844. Today the old mansion is a
landmark listed in the National Register
of Historic Places, and its restaurant
serves what the chef calls "French clas-
sical Bahamian cuisine." By combining
local foods, such as conch, grouper,
snapper, and spiny lobster, with island
spices and European cooking techniques, Graycliff has evolved into the
only five-star restaurant in the
Bahamas.*

Potato Salad

3 pounds unpeeled boiling
potatoes
Salt and freshly ground pepper
to taste
Garlic powder to taste
1/2 cup mayonnaise
3 tablespoons sweet pickle
relish
2 stalks celery, finely chopped
2 tablespoons cider vinegar
1 tablespoon dry mustard
4 scallions, finely chopped
4 hard-boiled eggs, chopped
1/2 green bell pepper, seeded,
deribbed, and chopped
2 tablespoons minced fresh dill
2 tablespoons minced fresh
parsley
Paprika for sprinkling

Serves 6

Potato salad is one of the great traveling foods, whether you carry it to a huge party, a family gathering, your godchild's graduation, a church meeting, or a picnic. From the very beginning, the idea of a picnic meant a meal where everyone brought something. Now, everybody knows that a picnic is not a picnic without potato salad. And as a Southerner, I say that potato salad ain't potato salad without eggs in it. Just be sure you keep this potato salad cold when you take it to your picnic.

Place the potatoes in a large saucepan and add water to cover. Bring to a boil, reduce the heat to a simmer, and cook until the potatoes are tender but not mushy, 20 to 30 minutes. Drain, rinse in cold water, and let cool to the touch. Peel the potatoes and cut them into 1/2-inch dice. While they are still warm, season the potatoes with salt, pepper, and garlic powder.

In another bowl, combine half of the mayonnaise with the relish, celery, vinegar, mustard, scallions, eggs, and bell pepper. Add to the potatoes and mix well. Taste and adjust the seasonings. Stir in more mayonnaise if you want, and half the dill and parsley. Refrigerate until cold. When ready to serve, check the seasonings again, adding more mayonnaise as needed and the rest of the dill and parsley. Sprinkle with paprika.

IT WAS THE INCAN INDIANS OF SOUTH America who developed the potato. Not only did they have many different varieties, they perfected the art of freeze-drying potatoes in their high-altitude kingdom.

Side Dishes and Breads

A Pot of Beans

2   cups dried pinto beans

3   quarts water

1   small onion, halved, plus 1
    medium onion, chopped

5   Mexican chorizo sausages,
    removed from casings and
    crumbled

4   cloves garlic, minced

1   small green bell pepper, seed-
    ed, deribbed, and chopped

3   jalapeño chilies, seeded and
    minced

    Salt and freshly ground pepper
    to taste

2   tomatoes, chopped

1/2 cup chopped fresh cilantro

    Serves 6

No Mexican meal is quite complete without beans and rice. In Mexico, beans are cooked many ways. One of the most basic is *frijoles de olla,* which means beans cooked in a big clay pot. The pot in this recipe is a regular stockpot, and the beans are pinto beans, but you can use almost any kind of bean instead. Make sure you pick over them carefully to remove any small stones.

Pick over and rinse the beans. Soak the beans in water to cover overnight. Rinse and place in a stockpot. Add the 3 quarts water and the halved onion. Bring to a boil, reduce the heat to low, and simmer until the beans are tender, about 1 1/2 hours.

In a skillet, combine the crumbled chorizo, garlic, chopped onion, and bell pepper and sauté over medium heat for a few minutes. Add the jalapeños, salt, and pepper. Pour off all but about 1 tablespoon of fat. Add the sausage mixture to the beans along with the tomatoes. Cover and cook for about 30 minutes, stirring occasionally and adding more water, if needed. Garnish with cilantro and serve.

COOKBOOKS AND COOKS GIVE MUCH advice on how to cook beans. There is the "don't soak overnight" school and the "must soak overnight" school. And there's the "don't add salt to the beans until they are done or they will be tough" school, and the "it doesn't matter when you add what school." I soak my beans overnight and salt them toward the end, but you are free to cook them any way you want. Just remember the Mexican proverb: "He who follows his own advice must take the consequences." On the other hand, don't be afraid to be adventuresome. There is another Mexican proverb that says: "He who does not venture has no luck."

Cuban Black Beans

2 cups dried black beans
1 large piece onion
1 large piece green bell pepper
1 teaspoon olive oil
1 teaspoon dry sherry
2 cloves garlic, crushed
1 bay leaf, crumbled
1 teaspoon each dried thyme, dried oregano, and ground cumin

Sofrito
1/4 cup olive oil
1 large yellow onion, diced
1 small green bell pepper, seeded, deribbed, and diced
6 to 8 cloves garlic, crushed
1 teaspoon dried basil, crumbled
1 teaspoon dried oregano, crumbled
1 teaspoon ground cumin
Salt and freshly ground pepper to taste

1 teaspoon sugar
2 tablespoons dry sherry
1 tablespoon distilled white vinegar
Salt and freshly ground pepper to taste
Ground cumin to taste

Serves 8 to 10

Like so many Cuban dishes, these black beans are flavored with *sofrito,* a sautéed mixture of bell pepper, onion, and garlic. Serve these over rice, or eat alone as a soup or stew.

Pick over and rinse the beans. In a stockpot, combine the beans with water to cover by 4 inches. Add the onion piece, bell pepper piece, olive oil, sherry, garlic, bay leaf, and herbs. Soak the beans overnight.

When ready to cook, do not drain the beans. Bring the pot of beans and water to a simmer, cover, and cook for 2 to 3 hours, stirring frequently and testing for doneness after 1 hour. Add small amounts of water only if needed. The beans should not be runny. Turn off the heat and set aside, or refrigerate overnight.

To make the sofrito: In a skillet over medium heat, heat the olive oil and cook the diced onion, diced bell pepper, and garlic until the onion is translucent, about 3 minutes. Add the basil, oregano, cumin, salt, and pepper.

Add the sofrito to the beans, cover, and cook for about 1 hour longer. Add the sugar, sherry, and vinegar. Season with salt, pepper, and cumin.

THE CARIBBEAN LOVE OF BEAN DISHES goes all the way back to the Arawak Indians, the indigenous people of Cuba and Hispaniola, who grew beans and corn, and harvested the abundant seafood, tropical fruit, and turtle eggs of the islands.

A-Taste-of-Home Peas and Coconut Rice

2 tablespoons vegetable oil
1 small onion, chopped
3 cloves garlic, minced
1/2 small green bell pepper,
    seeded, deribbed, and
    chopped
1 cup long-grain white rice
1 cup coconut milk
2 cups chicken broth
1 (16-ounce) can pigeon peas,
    black-eyed peas, or red
    beans, drained and rinsed
1 teaspoon dried thyme,
    crumbled
1 teaspoon dried oregano,
    crumbled
    Salt and freshly ground pepper
    to taste
    Red pepper flakes to taste

Serves 4 to 6

One hundred years after African Americans found refuge in Canada, descendants of former slaves from the Caribbean emigrated to the land of the maple leaf. They were from countries like Haiti, Trinidad, and Jamaica. They came with aspirations for a new life and with culinary memories. Eventually they adapted to the climate and customs of Canada, but they never forgot the tastes of home, like this Caribbean dish.

In a large saucepan over medium heat, heat the oil and sauté the onion, garlic, and bell pepper for 3 or 4 minutes. Add the rice and stir to coat with the oil for about 1 minute. Add the coconut milk and broth. Stir in all the remaining ingredients. Bring to a boil, reduce the heat to low, cover, and cook until the rice is tender, about 25 minutes.

Haitian Red Beans and Rice

1 cup dried red beans

5 cups water

2 tablespoons olive oil

1 onion, chopped

2 cloves garlic, minced

Large pinch of dried thyme, crumbled

Salt and freshly ground black pepper to taste

Cayenne pepper to taste

1 cup long-grain white rice

Serves 6 to 8

Grains have always been popular in Haiti. The native Arawak people cultivated corn. The Spanish brought wheat, as well as another grain that has become a staple in Haiti: rice. Nowadays there are several varieties of rice grown in the Caribbean—including Haiti—and it is prepared in several different ways. One dish is familiar to the rest of the Caribbean and the United States, particularly New Orleans: red beans and rice. Unlike the cooks of some rice and beans dishes, the Haitians cook the rice in the bean liquid, so make sure you sort and rinse the beans well.

Pick over and rinse the beans. Soak in water to cover overnight. Drain and cook in the 5 cups water until tender, about 1 hour. Drain, reserving the liquid.

In a stockpot over medium heat, heat the oil and sauté the onion and garlic for about 3 minutes. Add the beans, thyme, salt, black pepper, and cayenne pepper. Add the reserved bean liquid and bring to a boil. Stir in the rice and reduce the heat to low. Cover and simmer for 20 minutes, or until the rice is tender.

THE OTHER FRENCH CARIBBEAN ISLANDS are more French than African in heritage, but Haiti is African first, then French. You can see this in their cuisine, which retains more African ingredients and techniques than that of any other Caribbean island.

Jag

1/4 cup vegetable oil

1 large onion, chopped

2 1/2 cups water

Salt and freshly ground black
    pepper or red pepper flakes
    to taste

2 bay leaves

1/2 teaspoon dried thyme,
    crumbled

1/2 cup puréed tomatoes

1 (15-ounce) can kidney beans,
    rinsed and drained

1 cup long-grain white rice

Serves 4 to 6

If you were raised in a Cape Verdean home or are fortunate enough to call a Cape Verdean your friend, then you're probably familiar with *jagacida,* or *jag,* a popular rice and bean dish that can be served either as a side dish or as a meal in itself.

Now, like all recipes that have a bit of history behind them, you will find some creative play with the ingredients. This dish can be made with or without tomatoes. Some like it red, and some don't. Cape Verdeans serve this dish with chicken or *linguiça,* a nice Portuguese sausage, but you can pick any other meat that you wish. It's just delicious.

In a saucepan over medium heat, heat the oil and sauté the onion for 3 or 4 minutes. Add the water, salt, pepper, bay leaves, thyme, tomatoes, and beans. Bring to a boil and stir in the rice. Reduce the heat to low, cover, and simmer for about 25 minutes, or until the rice is tender. Remove and discard the bay leaves before serving.

Haitian Rice with Black Mushrooms

(A Wannabe Riz Djon Djon)

3 tablespoons dried shiitake
   mushrooms

1 cup boiling water

1 thick slice bacon, chopped

2 scallions, chopped, including
   green portions

Minced Scotch bonnet chili to
   taste

2 cloves garlic, minced

1 cup long-grain white rice

1 cup chicken broth or vegetable
   broth

Salt and freshly ground pepper
   to taste

Serves 4 to 6

Like red beans and rice, *riz djon djon* is very popular in Haiti. It's made with dried black mushrooms that grow wild only in the cool mountains of Haiti. You can probably find some *djon djon* mushrooms in a specialty grocery store, or you might get some from a Haitian friend. But if you can't, dried shiitakes are a good substitute. Like *djon djons,* they add a rich intensity to the taste and look of this rice dish.

Place the mushrooms in a bowl, cover with the boiling water, and let stand until they are softened, about 20 minutes. Remove the mushrooms, reserving the soaking liquid. Pour the soaking liquid through a paper coffee filter. Squeeze the mushrooms over the bowl to dry them a little. Remove and discard the tough mushroom stems and chop the mushrooms. Set aside.

Fry the bacon until crisp. Using a slotted spoon, transfer the bacon to paper towels to drain. Add the scallions and chili to the bacon fat and sauté for 1 minute. Add the garlic and sauté for another minute. Add the rice and stir for 1 minute. Add the mushroom soaking liquid, broth, salt, and pepper. Bring to a boil, reduce the heat to low, cover, and cook until the rice is tender, 15 to 17 minutes. Remove from the heat and let the rice stand, covered, for a few minutes. Gently stir the rice with a fork to fluff and to distribute the other ingredients and serve.

Acelgas con Limon

(Swiss Chard with Lemon)

1 tablespoon olive oil

2 bunches Swiss chard, cut into
  thin shreds

2 tablespoons unsalted butter

1 tablespoon all-purpose flour

  Juice of 1 large lemon

  Salt and freshly ground pepper
  to taste

1/4 cup water

  Croutons (see introduction),
  optional

Serves 4

Dudley Nieto, the chef at Blue Mesa Restaurant in Chicago, gave me this Mexican recipe for Swiss chard in a lemony sauce. It's even better with homemade croutons. Just mince a clove garlic and sauté it in a little olive oil and butter over medium heat. Add a handful of cubed bread and stir until golden brown and crisp. Sprinkle the croutons over the chard and serve right away for a delightful contrast in textures and tastes.

In a large skillet over medium heat, heat the olive oil and sauté the chard for 2 or 3 minutes, or until it begins to wilt. Cover the pan and cook for about 5 more minutes, or until the chard is tender. Pour the chard into a colander and press the moisture out with the back of a large spoon. Set aside.

In a large saucepan, melt the butter over medium-low heat. Add the flour and stir constantly for 1 or 2 minutes. Add the lemon juice, salt, pepper, and water. Continue to cook, stirring constantly, until thickened. Taste and adjust the seasonings. Stir in the chard and heat for a few minutes. Serve at once, topped with croutons, if using.

Corn on the Cob with Chili Butter

1/2 cup unsalted butter at room
    temperature
1 tablespoon ground pure red
    chili (not chili powder)
  Salt to taste
6 fresh ears of corn, husks and
    silk removed
  Lime wedges, for serving

Serves 6

Corn is American! At the time of Cortez, it is said that corn was so plentiful that it was planted by the sides of roads for hungry travelers. In Oaxaca, I had the best corn ever. I was in a restaurant waiting for some people and decided to take a walk around the square. I bought an ear of corn from a vendor to ease my hunger. Well, the corn was so good...It was grilled over charcoal, splashed with butter, rolled in chili powder, and sprinkled with lime juice. What a taste. I ate so many I hardly had room for dinner. Since then, I always have chili butter on my corn. So boil or grill your corn, but try this! Chili butter is also great on grilled or broiled fish.

Cream the butter by hand in a bowl until light and fluffy. Add the ground chili and salt. Refrigerate for at least 1 hour to blend the flavors. Boil the corn for about 5 minutes or grill until lightly browned all over. Spread with the chili butter, serve with lime wedges, and eat right away.

Creamed Corn

3 cups fresh or frozen corn
    kernels
3/4 cup heavy cream, plus more
    as needed
3 saffron threads
  Salt and freshly ground white
    pepper to taste

Serves 4 to 6

You can make this dish, from Leonne Reynold, of the Hotel Villa Creole in Port-au-Prince, with frozen corn, but to be at its heavenly best it should be made with fresh sweet corn. This is good with anything, but especially with fried and grilled foods. The addition of saffron is literally brilliant because it makes the corn a golden yellow.

Cook the corn in salted boiling water for 5 minutes. Drain. Meanwhile, heat the cream in a small pan until bubbles form around the edges. Stir in the saffron until dissolved. In a blender or food processor, purée the corn and cream mixture, adding a little more cream if necessary. Or, you could use a food mill, or force the mixture through a coarse-meshed sieve with the back of a large spoon. Stir in the salt and pepper. Serve warm.

One characteristic of Haitian cookery is that it makes use of everything. As the Haitians say, "When you're starved, a potato has no peel." In other words, nothing is wasted.

Corn Squares

4 tablespoons unsalted butter
2 cloves garlic, minced
1 onion, finely chopped
4 cups water
1 tablespoon salt, plus salt to
   taste
3 cups cornmeal
3 cups milk
3/4 cup coconut milk
3/4 cup heavy cream
1 cup grated Parmesan cheese
   Freshly ground white pepper
   to taste
1 egg, beaten with 1 tablespoon
   water
   Vegetable oil, for frying

Serves 6 to 8

She just calls them corn squares, but this dish by Leonne Reynold, who is the head chef for the Hotel Villa Creole in Port-au-Prince, Haiti, is some kind of exquisite take on fried polenta, except with a tropical twist. You won't believe how good these are.

In a large, heavy saucepan, melt the butter over medium heat and sauté the garlic and onion until translucent, about 3 minutes. Add the water and the 1 tablespoon salt and bring to a boil. Gradually whisk in the cornmeal. Reduce the heat to a simmer and cook, uncovered, for 5 minutes. Stir in the milk and cook for 5 minutes. Stir in the coconut milk and simmer, stirring occasionally, until thickened, about 10 minutes. Stir in the cream and 1/2 cup of the Parmesan. Season with pepper and salt to taste.

Pour the mixture into a well-oiled 12 x 9-inch baking dish. Spread it evenly and smooth the surface with a wet rubber spatula. Refrigerate for 30 minutes. Cut into squares with a wet knife. Remove a square using a metal spatula. Dip the square in the beaten egg, then in the remaining Parmesan. Repeat to dip all the remaining squares.

In a large skillet over medium heat, heat about 1/4 inch of the oil until fragrant. Add several dipped squares, making sure not to crowd them. Cook for 3 or 4 minutes on each side, or until golden brown. Using a metal spatula, transfer to a baking sheet and place in a low oven to keep the squares warm. Repeat to cook the remaining squares. Serve at once.

Yuca with Mojo Sauce

14 to 16 ounces frozen yuca
(cassava)
1 teaspoon salt

Mojo Sauce
1/4 cup olive oil
Cloves from 1 head garlic,
sliced
1/4 cup freshly squeezed lime
juice
Salt and freshly ground pepper
to taste

Hot pepper sauce, for serving

Serves 4

In the neighborhoods where I've lived, yuca is not an exotic and strange ingredient. Ever since I had my first kitchen of my own, I've lived in neighborhoods where you can buy yuca and plantains and other foods like that. The mojo sauce is garlic fried in olive oil, and you put the spicy sauce over the yuca, a root that cooks up bland and soft, like a potato. Be sure not to let the garlic burn.

Place the yuca in a large saucepan and add the 1 teaspoon salt and water to cover. Bring the water to a boil and cook the yuca until tender, about 20 minutes. Drain and cut into pieces.

To make the sauce: In a small saucepan over medium-low heat, heat the oil and sauté the garlic until golden brown. Add the lime juice, salt, and pepper.

Pour the sauce over the yuca and serve.

THE ORIGINAL INHABITANTS OF CUBA, the Arawak Indians, learned to make the native yuca edible by first peeling it, then grating it and putting it through a sieve. This step was necessary to remove the poisonous juices of wild yuca. The yuca that now is cultivated for consumption has had these juices bred out of it, and is safe to eat.

Red Polenta

1 cup dried red kidney beans
2 tablespoons peanut oil or
   olive oil
2 cloves garlic, crushed
   Minced Scotch bonnet chili
   to taste
1 cup polenta
3 to 4 tablespoons unsalted
   butter
   Salt to taste

Serves 6

I love this simple and wonderful dish. I first had it at the home of my friend, the glamorous actress Josephine Premice. Josephine is Haitian, and at her elegant table, I was introduced to numerous Creole dishes. But the flavor memory that stays with me is the taste of a time-honored peasant dish, a blend of cornmeal and red kidney beans, which Ms. Josephine served on Limoges china. This is my adaptation. Because of Josephine's elegant presentation, I call it Red Polenta. If you want to use canned beans, use 4 cups, rinsed and drained, and add them at the end.

Pick over and rinse the beans. Soak in water to cover overnight. Drain and cook the beans in water to cover until tender, about 1 hour. Drain, reserving the liquid. Add water to the reserved stock as needed to make 4 cups liquid. In a skillet over medium heat, heat the oil and fry the beans, garlic, and chili for about 5 minutes. Set aside.

In a heavy pot, mix the polenta with 1 cup of the reserved bean liquid until blended. Add the remaining bean liquid and stir until blended. Bring to a boil, reduce the heat to low, and cook, stirring very frequently, until thick, about 40 minutes. Stir in the bean mixture, butter, and salt. Serve hot.

THE FOOD OF HAITI IS A DELICIOUS AND spicy blend of ingredients, a cultural stew. The recipe? Simple. One part Native American, one part European, one part African. Mix together and simmer for, oh, at least three or four hundred years. Then, voilà! Creole cooking that can't be beat.

Plantains with Cheese Sauce

1/4 cup canola oil

3 ripe plantains, peeled and
   sliced lengthwise

4 tablespoons unsalted butter

1/4 cup all purpose flour

2 1/2 cups milk

   Pinch of ground nutmeg

   Salt and freshly ground pepper
   to taste

1 cup shredded Monterey jack
   cheese

1 cup shredded Cheddar cheese

Serves 6

There is a continuum of vegetarianism. There are people who don't eat red meat, but do eat fish, poultry, and dairy products. At the other end of the spectrum are vegans—those who don't eat meat, fish, or fowl, eggs, or dairy—no animal products at all. In the middle are those who eat no meat, fish, or poultry, but do like their eggs and dairy: This dish is for them. (And for nonvegetarians, this is a wonderful side dish with grilled meats.)

Preheat the oven to 350°. In a large skillet over medium heat, heat the oil and brown the plantains on both sides. Using a slotted metal spatula, transfer the plantains to a plate lined with paper towels to drain. Keep warm in a low oven while making the cheese sauce.

In a saucepan, melt the butter over low heat. Add the flour and stir for 2 minutes. Gradually whisk in the milk. Add the nutmeg, salt, and pepper. Cook, whisking constantly, until thickened. Stir in the cheeses and cook, stirring constantly, until the cheeses melt.

Lay the plantain slices on a platter or on individual serving dishes, spoon the cheese sauce over the top, and serve immediately.

PLANTAINS ARE RELATED TO BANANAS and taste like bananas, especially when fully ripe, but their flesh is much starchier and they can't be eaten raw. (They are full of tannin, the same stuff that causes unripe persimmons to make your mouth pucker.) Green plantains are firm and so are especially good for frying, because they don't fall apart, but you can also use yellow plantains spotted with black. A completely ripe plantain will be almost black.

Chayote in Cheese Sauce

1 large chayote, peeled and cut
   into 1/2-inch dice
2 tablespoons unsalted butter
2 tablespoons all purpose flour
1 cup milk
1/2 cup grated Monterey jack
   cheese
1/2 teaspoon salt
   Dash of cayenne pepper

Serves 4

Chayote, one of the most important vegetables in Latin American cuisine, is also eaten throughout the Deep South. Mexican chef Dudley Nieto remembers his grandmother, Virginia Romero, saying that the chayote has curative powers for liver, kidney, and urinary tract problems. This is his recipe.

Cook the chayote in salted boiling water until tender, 10 to 15 minutes. Drain and set aside. In a saucepan, melt the butter over medium-low heat. Stir in the flour and cook, stirring constantly, for 2 minutes. Gradually whisk in the milk and cook, whisking constantly, until thickened. Stir in the cheese until melted. Add the salt and cayenne. Stir in the cooked chayote and cook for 2 or 3 minutes, or until heated through.

THE CHAYOTE, ALSO CALLED CHOCHO *and* mirliton, *was an important food to the Aztecs and Mayas. Today it is eaten throughout Mexico, Central America,* *the Caribbean, and the American South. Because of its mild taste, it takes well to flavorful sauces and assertive seasonings.*

Coconut Sweet Potatoes

4 small sweet potatoes
1 tablespoon unsalted butter
1 tablespoon peanut or canola
  oil
1/2 cup coconut cream
1/4 cup packed brown sugar

Serves 4

I love this way of cooking sweet potatoes, adapted from a recipe in my first book, *Vibration Cooking*. The coconut cream and brown sugar are a divine combination with the sweet potatoes. You could sprinkle the dish with some grated coconut, if you want. Serve this at your next Thanksgiving dinner, and your guests will be truly thankful.

Cook the sweet potatoes in boiling water to cover for 20 minutes. Drain and let cool to the touch, then peel and cut into $5/8$-inch-thick slices. In a large skillet, melt the butter with the oil over medium-low heat. Add the sweet potato slices and cook until lightly browned on each side. Add the coconut cream and brown sugar. Cover and cook until tender, about 10 minutes.

Dawn Applesauce

4 apples, peeled, cored, and
   coarsely chopped
1 cup water
3/4 cup sugar
   Juice of 1 lemon
1/4 teaspoon ground cinnamon
   Pinch of salt

Makes 2 to 3 cups

I'm inviting you to breakfast at Dawn. Dawn is across the river from Motown, in Dresden, Ontario. Ontario is the apple-growing region of Canada. A man named Josiah Henson, born a slave in Maryland, escaped to Canada in 1830. In 1841, Henson and a group of abolitionists purchased two hundred acres of land and established a settlement named Dawn. They established the British-American Institute for Fugitive Slaves; built a vocational school, a sawmill, and a gristmill; raised livestock and chickens; and grew their own crops. Dawn became a home to fugitive slaves, brought from the United States on the Underground Railroad, the "train with no tracks."

Imagine that first breakfast in freedom, sitting down to a plate of bacon, sausages, and scrapple from the smokehouse; soft scrambled fresh eggs from the henhouse; and sweet potato pancakes drenched with maple syrup, with a side of chunky applesauce made from sweet apples from the orchard.

Combine the apples, water, sugar, and lemon juice in a saucepan. Bring to a boil, reduce the heat to low, cover, and simmer until the apples are tender, about 15 minutes. Stir occasionally and check to make sure there is enough water to keep the apples from sticking. Add more water if it's too thick. Remove from the heat and mash with the back of a wooden spoon. Keep the sauce on the chunky side. Stir in the cinnamon and salt. Let cool.

JOSIAH HENSON TRAVELED TO NEW YORK and New England, telling of his life in slavery. On one of these trips, he visited Harriet Beecher Stowe in Andover, Massachusetts, and the details of his slavery experience are said to have inspired her to write Uncle Tom's Cabin. *The donations that Henson received for his speeches benefited the settlement of Dawn. Today, Dawn has been declared a historic site.*

Buttermilk Biscuits

2 cups all-purpose flour
2 teaspoons baking powder
1/4 teaspoon baking soda
1/8 teaspoon salt
4 tablespoons cold unsalted
  butter
1 cup buttermilk

Makes about 16 biscuits

This is an adaptation of the biscuit recipe from my first book, *Vibration Cooking.* These can be whipped up in no time, and you can't imagine how much your guests will appreciate hot homemade biscuits. Serve them with butter and honey or preserves.

Preheat the oven to 375°. Grease a heavy baking sheet or line it with parchment paper. In a bowl, stir the flour, baking powder, baking soda, and salt together. Cut in the butter with a pastry cutter or rub it in with your fingers until the mixture is the texture of coarse crumbs. Gradually stir in the buttermilk to make a stiff dough.

On a lightly floured board, knead the dough for 2 or 3 minutes, or until smooth. Pinch off pieces of dough the size of golf balls, forming each into a thick disk. Or, if you prefer, roll the dough out about 3/4-inch thick and cut with a biscuit cutter. Place the biscuits on the prepared pan and bake until golden brown, about 10 minutes.

WHEN I LEARNED TO MAKE BUTTERMILK biscuits as a child, I never dreamed that I would one day be making them for a Hollywood movie. As culinary consultant for Beloved, *I rolled and cut more biscuits than you could count with Oprah in her biscuit-making scene. Working with her, the director Jonathan Demme, and the rest of the cast was a real highlight of my life.*

Sweet Potato-Corn Muffins

3 slices bacon
3/4 cup all-purpose flour
11/2 cups yellow cornmeal
2 teaspoons baking powder
1 tablespoon sugar
Pinch of salt
1 egg, slightly beaten
1/4 cup vegetable oil
1 cup mashed sweet potato
1/2 cup buttermilk, plus more as
needed

Makes 1 dozen muffins

In France during the Middle Ages, Notre Dame Cathedral sponsored a pork sale. This pig fair was known as a *bacon,* which is where we get the name for a favorite breakfast meat, also used as a seasoning in many different foods. Here's a bread that gets some of its flavor from bacon.

Preheat the oven to 350°. Grease 12 standard muffin cups and place in the oven to heat. In a skillet, cook the bacon until crisp. Drain on paper towels, crumble, and set aside in a bowl.

In a large bowl, stir the flour, cornmeal, baking powder, sugar, and salt together. In a medium bowl, mix the egg, oil, sweet potato, and 1/2 cup buttermilk together. Stir the wet ingredients into the dry ingredients just until blended; the batter should be slightly lumpy. Add another 1 or 2 tablespoons of buttermilk if the dough seems too stiff. Gently fold in the bacon. Spoon into the prepared muffin cups. Bake for about 25 minutes, or until the muffins are browned.

Black Pepper Corn Bread

2 tablespoons unsalted butter, melted
1 cup white cornmeal
1 cup all-purpose flour
1 tablespoon sugar
1 tablespoon baking powder
1 teaspoon baking soda
1 teaspoon salt
1/2 cup cold cooked grits
1 1/2 cups buttermilk
1 large egg
1/2 teaspoon freshly ground black pepper, or more to taste

Serves 6

This is a very special recipe. It's my riff, but the dish was created by my dear friend the late Bill Neal and served at his restaurant, Crooks Corner, in Chapel Hill, North Carolina. The original recipe is in Bill's book, *Grits.* Adding the cold grits is what gives this corn bread its unique texture and—along with the pepper—makes it different from traditional Southern corn bread.

Preheat the oven to 400°. Brush a 10-inch round glass pie pan with some of the butter and place in the oven to heat.

In a large bowl, stir the cornmeal, flour, sugar, baking powder, baking soda, and salt together. In a medium bowl, beat the grits, the remaining butter, buttermilk, and egg together until smooth. Pour into the flour mixture and stir just until blended; do not overmix. Pour the batter into the prepared pan. Sprinkle the black pepper on top.

Place the pie plate in the oven and reduce the temperature to 350°. Bake the corn bread until the top is lightly browned and the center is set, about 25 minutes. Let cool for a few minutes before removing from the pan.

ONE VARIETY OF WHITE CORN IS CALLED hominy. Being a child of the South, I have a special appreciation for hominy, which is used to make grits, a traditional part of any good Southern breakfast. This is one of the many areas where Native American and African cultures have blended in the South. Often, Native Americans would open up their villages to runaway slaves. Some, like the Florida Seminoles, were runaways themselves. Along with our shared journeys, we shared our ways of cooking—the Native Americans with the indigenous foods of the New World, and the ex-slaves with their long memories of African cooking methods, adapting them to the cattle and pigs brought over by the Europeans.

Skillet Corn Bread

2 cups white or yellow stone-
    ground cornmeal
1 teaspoon baking soda
1 teaspoon salt
1 teaspoon baking powder
1 egg
1 cup buttermilk

Serves 6

It needs to be repeated—as I do, over and over again—that the two secrets to making good corn bread are that you need a cast-iron skillet and you need to preheat it in the oven so it will be hot when you put the batter in. A cold skillet does *not* good corn bread make. This recipe is also in my book *Vertamae Cooks;* I'm repeating it here because it's such a good and basic recipe.

Preheat the oven to 450°. Lightly grease a 9-inch cast-iron skillet with butter and place it in the oven.

In a medium bowl, stir together the cornmeal, baking soda, salt, and baking powder. In a large bowl, beat the egg until blended, then stir in the buttermilk. Add the cornmeal mixture and stir just until there are no lumps; do not overmix.

Remove the preheated skillet from the oven and pour the batter into it. The batter should sizzle as it hits the hot pan. If it doesn't, your pan wasn't hot enough; remember to preheat it fully next time. Slip the skillet back into the oven and bake until the top is golden brown and crusty, about 25 minutes. Serve hot from the skillet.

Navajo Fry Bread

2 cups all-purpose flour, plus
    flour for dusting
1 tablespoon baking powder
1 teaspoon salt
1 tablespoon vegetable oil
3/4 cup warm water
    Corn oil, for deep-frying
    Powdered sugar for dusting,
        honey for drizzling, or honey
        butter for spreading

Makes 12 bread rounds

Here's a recipe for fry bread from *I Hear America Cooking,* by Betty Fussell. It's a close relative to sopaipillas, which are served in restaurants all over New Mexico just like bread is everywhere else. Navajo fry bread, though, is round, not square, and has a hole poked in the middle to help the dough cook evenly. It's easy to make, and so good when it's served right after you cook it.

In a bowl, stir the 2 cups flour, baking powder, and salt together. Stir in the oil and water until smooth. On a floured board, knead the dough for about 1 minute, until smooth. Form into a ball, wrap in plastic, and refrigerate for 1 hour.

Divide the dough into 12 pieces and roll each into a 3- to 4-inch round. Roll again to make the rounds as thin as possible, 7 to 8 inches in diameter; the thinner they are, the better they will puff in the oil. Poke a hole in the center of each round with your finger.

In a large Dutch oven or deep fryer, heat about 3 inches of oil to 375°. Meanwhile, lightly dust the tops of the dough rounds with flour. Slip the rounds one at a time into the oil in batches so the pan is not crowded, cooking them for about 1 minute on each side, or until browned. Using tongs or a slotted spatula, transfer to paper towels to drain. Keep warm in a low oven while cooking the remaining rounds. Dust the hot rounds with powdered sugar, drizzle honey over them, or spread with honey butter. Serve at once.

THE NATIVE AMERICANS OF THE Southwest got their flour and sugar from the Spanish in the early sixteenth century. Before that, they used corn-meal and honey for their sweet breads. Sopaipilla is a Spanish word for one kind of deep-fried bread, shaped like little pillows. It's a little more sophisticated than fry bread, which is found at street stands and powwows. Both remind me of the fried breads you get in New Orleans.

Coconut Bread

4 cups all-purpose flour
2 teaspoons baking powder
1/2 teaspoon salt
1 egg
3/4 cup milk
1/2 cup unsalted butter, melted
1 teaspoon vanilla extract
1/2 cup packed brown sugar, plus
    2 packed tablespoons for
    dusting
2 cups shredded dried coconut
1/2 cup raisins, mixed with
    1 tablespoon flour

Makes 2 loaves

This is really a multipurpose bread. You can serve it as a snack, with tea or coffee, or you can serve it with an entrée, or with fruit as a dessert. Some Caribbean restaurants serve a bread basket with coconut bread and other sweet breads, like banana or date. It's also good toasted in the morning, with honey or jam.

Preheat the oven to 350°. Grease two 9 x 5-inch loaf pans. In a medium bowl, stir the flour, baking powder, and salt together. In a large bowl, beat the egg. Whisk in the milk, melted butter, and vanilla. Stir in the 1/2 cup brown sugar and the flour mixture. Fold in the coconut and raisins.

On a lightly floured board, knead the dough for a few quick strokes. Divide the dough in two and form each piece into a loaf. Place each loaf in a prepared pan. Dust each loaf with 1 tablespoon brown sugar by pushing the sugar through a sieve with the back of a spoon. Bake for about 1 hour, or until each loaf springs back when lightly pressed.

Easter Spice Bun

1 egg

1 1/2 cups packed brown sugar

2 tablespoons unsalted butter, melted

1 cup milk or dry white wine

2 1/2 cups all-purpose flour

4 teaspoons baking powder

1 teaspoon ground nutmeg

1 teaspoon ground cinnamon

Pinch of salt

1 cup raisins

1 teaspoon freshly squeezed lime juice

1/4 cup Myers's rum

Glaze (optional)

1/2 cup packed brown sugar

1/2 cup water

Makes one 9 x 5-inch loaf

While staying in Paris, one of the things that I missed most was the down-home cooking of the South. I would see people greeting their loved ones with a container full of their favorite native foods as they arrived in town. When any of my friends or relatives came to Paris, I made sure they brought some grits and black-eyed peas. I almost felt like I was back in Carolina. I'm sure that Jamaican and Caribbean immigrants know how I felt. This bun, served with cheese, is a traditional Easter dish, and post offices and even airports receive an abundance of parcels with buns for out-of-town relatives wherever they may be. This bun (which is really a loaf) has now become popular all over the world. After making it, you'll know why.

You can use several different types of leavening agents for this bun, like yeast, baking soda, or stout, but my personal preference is baking powder because it's reliable and easy.

Preheat the oven to 350°. Line the bottom of a 9 x 5-inch loaf pan with waxed paper. Grease the paper and sides and dust with flour; tap out the excess.

In a medium bowl, beat the egg and sugar together until blended. Stir in the melted butter and milk or wine. In a large bowl, stir the flour, baking powder, nutmeg, cinnamon, and salt together. Pour the wet ingredients into the dry ingredients and stir just until smooth. Stir in the raisins, lime juice, and rum. Pour into the prepared pan and bake for about 1 hour, or until a skewer inserted in the center comes out clean.

If you are making the glaze, start it while the bun is baking. In a small saucepan, stir the brown sugar and water together until the sugar is dissolved. Bring to a boil, reduce the heat to a simmer, and cook, stirring constantly, until thick. When the bun is done, spread the glaze over it and pop it back in the oven for about 5 minutes, or until the glaze bubbles.

Entrées

Buffalo Chili

1¹/2 pounds buffalo or beef stew
 meat, cut into ¹/2-inch dice
1¹/2 pounds ground pork
 Salt to taste
¹/4 teaspoon freshly ground black
 pepper
 All-purpose flour, for dredging
3 tablespoons olive oil
1 large onion, chopped
5 cloves garlic, crushed
1 tablespoon ground cumin
3 tablespoons ground pure red
 chili (not chili powder), or
 more to taste
1 teaspoon dried sage, crumbled
1 teaspoon dried thyme,
 crumbled
1 teaspoon dried oregano,
 crumbled
1 (16-ounce) can puréed Italian
 (plum) tomatoes
¹/2 cup beef stock or water, plus
 more as needed
¹/4 cup tomato paste

 Serves 8 to 10

Ground pork has been added to this Native American dish because buffalo meat is not marbled with fat, and contrary to what might be the culinary trend, you need some fat for flavor and to keep the meat moist. This chili is made without beans.

Season the buffalo or beef and pork meat with salt and pepper. Dredge the meat in flour. In a cast-iron pot or a Dutch oven over medium heat, heat the oil and sauté the meat until browned. Spoon off the fat. Add the onion, garlic, spices, and herbs. Add the tomatoes, stock or water, and tomato paste and bring to a boil. Reduce the heat to low, cover, and simmer, stirring occasionally, for 1¹/2 to 2 hours, or until the meat is tender. Taste and adjust the seasonings.

BUFFALO MEAT IS SIMILAR TO BEEF, except that it is leaner. When Christopher Columbus arrived here it is said the buffalo population on the Great Plains was 125 million. For Native Americans, the buffalo was the symbol of the Great Spirit and was a culinary treasure that could be turned into jerky and be carried with them on journeys.

At the turn of this century it was reported there were only a few hundred buffalo left. Remember Buffy St. Marie's haunting song, "Now That the Buffalo's Gone"? Well, the buffalo's back. They are farm-raised in Montana, the Dakotas, Idaho, Colorado, California, and Texas.

Picadillo with Vegetables

1 pound ground beef
1 large onion, diced
1 green bell pepper, seeded,
      deribbed, and diced
5 cloves garlic, minced
   Salt and freshly ground black
      pepper to taste
2 tomatoes, chopped
3 chayotes, peeled and diced
3 carrots, peeled and diced
   About 10 pimiento-stuffed
      green olives, sliced
1 teaspoon dried thyme,
      crumbled
1 teaspoon ground cumin
   Cayenne pepper to taste
1/4 cup chopped fresh cilantro,
      plus more for garnish

Serves 6

Picadillo, a descendant of a Moorish dish, is a meat and vegetable hash eaten throughout Latin America and sometimes used as a filling for empanadas and other dishes. This is a Cuban version of picadillo. Serve it over rice, with Cuban Black Beans (page 42) and Yuca with Mojo Sauce (page 52).

In a large, heavy skillet, cook the meat over medium heat until browned. Pour off the excess fat. Add the onion, bell pepper, and garlic and sauté for 3 or 4 minutes. Add all the remaining ingredients except the cilantro. Cover and cook for 30 to 40 minutes. Add the 1/4 cup cilantro and cook a few more minutes. Sprinkle with more cilantro and serve.

Rabo Encendido

(Oxtail Stew)

3 to 4 pounds oxtails, cut into
    2-inch pieces
  Salt and freshly ground black
    pepper to taste
  Garlic powder to taste
  All-purpose flour for dredging
6 tablespoons olive oil
1 large onion, chopped
1 green bell pepper, seeded,
    deribbed, and chopped
5 cloves garlic, minced
1 cup chopped fresh cilantro
1 cup chopped tomatoes
1 teaspoon ground cumin
$1/2$ teaspoon dried oregano,
    crumbled
1 teaspoon dried thyme,
    crumbled
1 bay leaf
  Juice of 1 lime
1 cup dry red wine
2 to 3 cups water or beef stock
3 potatoes, peeled and
    quartered
2 carrots, peeled and cut into
    1-inch pieces

Serves 8 to 10

When I lived in New York, there were a number of Chinese Cuban restaurants in my neighborhood. The food was great, and the prices were right. Just $5.95 would get you an entrée and enough rice and beans to take home. The succulent spicy oxtails were my favorite. Although there were Chinese Cuban restaurants in the Bronx, Chelsea, Queens, and Brooklyn, I don't think there were any in Chinatown. And the menu wasn't a blend. You ordered Chinese or Cuban. It was on the same plate, but it wasn't a fusion.

Season the oxtails with salt, pepper, and garlic powder and dredge them in flour. In a heavy pot, heat 4 tablespoons of the olive oil and brown the oxtails on all sides. Remove the oxtails and discard the oil. Add the remaining 2 tablespoons oil and sauté the onion, bell pepper, and garlic for 3 to 5 minutes. Return the oxtails to the pot and add half of the cilantro and all the remaining ingredients except the potatoes and carrots. Bring to a boil, reduce the heat to low, cover, and simmer for $1^{1}/2$ to 2 hours, or until tender, adding more stock if needed. Add the remaining cilantro, the potatoes, and carrots. Cover and cook another 20 to 30 minutes, or until the vegetables are tender. Remove and discard the bay leaf before serving.

Avenue A Chicken

1   tablespoon unsalted butter
1   tablespoon olive oil
1   chicken, cut into serving
      pieces
1   large onion, chopped
1/2 green or red bell pepper,
      seeded, deribbed, and
      chopped
1   stalk celery, chopped
2   to 3 cloves garlic, minced
1/4 cup pimiento-stuffed green
      olives, sliced
1   small jar chopped pimientos
1   (14-ounce) can chopped toma-
      toes with juice
1/2 teaspoon paprika
     Salt and freshly ground pepper
      to taste

     Serves 4

I started making this chicken dish when I lived on Avenue A in New York. It quickly became a family favorite. It tastes best made the day before. Whenever my daughter Kali gets nostalgic for New York, she comes over and begs me to make Avenue A Chicken. Serve this over rice and with a green salad. It's wonderful.

In a large skillet over medium heat, melt the butter with the olive oil. Add the chicken and brown on both sides. Transfer the chicken to a plate. Add the onion, bell pepper, celery, and garlic to the pan and sauté for 3 or 4 minutes. Stir in the olives, pimientos, tomatoes, and paprika. Return the chicken to the pan and season with salt and pepper. Cover, reduce the heat to low, and cook until the chicken is tender, about 35 to 40 minutes, turning the chicken once or twice.

IN THE SOUTH, THE CHICKEN USED TO be called the gospel bird. Some say it was called that because for so many years, chicken was the centerpiece of the Southern Sunday dinner. But some say it's called the gospel bird because when the preacher came to dinner, he always got the best parts.

Baked Jerk Chicken

1 chicken, cut into serving
     pieces, or 4 chicken breasts
1 jar jerk sauce
     Olive oil, for coating

Serves 4

You've probably heard of the Jamaican preparation called jerk. No one knows where the name *jerk* comes from, but one explanation is that jerk seasoning is so spicy and hot that it makes your body jerk when you take a bite of any food made with it. This is a simple recipe for jerk chicken that I came across. Now, we're baking this chicken, but traditionally in Jamaica they cook jerk chicken over a grill using pimiento wood. But if you can't grill, this is one way of having a little jerk chicken.

Cut gashes in the chicken pieces or breasts with a large sharp knife. Using a teaspoon, fill the gashes with the jerk sauce. Brush the chicken with the olive oil, then spread more jerk sauce on both sides of each piece of chicken.

Place the chicken in a glass baking dish, cover, and refrigerate for 2 to 3 hours. Remove the chicken from the refrigerator 30 minutes before baking. Preheat the oven to 375°. Uncover and bake the chicken for about 55 minutes, or until the juices run clear and the chicken is crisp.

IN THE NINETEENTH CENTURY, MAROONS— runaway slaves in Jamaica—used a complex combination of seasonings to preserve the meats and foods they needed to survive without refrigeration. The seasonings in jerk included scallions, pepper, salt, brown sugar, pimiento, thyme, vinegar, cinnamon, garlic, and ginger. Some cooks claim to use over twenty different ingredients for their own special jerk sauces.

African Sweet Potato Stew

3¹/2 pounds sweet potatoes, peeled
and cubed

2 tablespoons vegetable oil

1 onion, chopped

3 cloves garlic, minced

1 teaspoon grated fresh ginger

1 stalk celery, chopped

1¹/2 cups chopped cabbage

1 cup chopped tomatoes

2 cups tomato juice

¹/2 teaspoon dried thyme,
crumbled

¹/2 teaspoon red pepper flakes
Salt and freshly ground black
pepper to taste

8 ounces vegetarian sausage,
sliced and cooked according
to directions on package

1 cup green beans, snapped and
cooked

¹/4 cup peanut butter

1 cup vegetable broth
Steamed rice, for serving

Serves 6

A good vegetarian stew with crusty bread and a hearty salad can be a satisfying meal even for nonvegetarians. This stew is very filling. The combination of sweet potatoes, peanuts, and vegetables is very prevalent in African cooking.

Cook the sweet potatoes in salted boiling water until tender, 20 to 30 minutes. Drain. Mash one fourth of the sweet potatoes. In a large skillet, heat the oil and sauté the onion, garlic, and ginger for about 5 minutes. Add the celery and cabbage and cook for about 3 minutes. Add the mashed and whole sweet potatoes, tomatoes, tomato juice, thyme, red pepper flakes, salt, and black pepper. Reduce the heat to low, cover, and simmer for about 10 minutes. Add the veggie sausages, green beans, and peanut butter. Add the vegetable broth. Cover and simmer for about 20 minutes. Taste and adjust the seasonings. Simmer for 10 more minutes. Serve over rice.

Oaxacan Marketplace Chicken

Juice of 2 lemons
8 tablespoons olive oil
10 cloves garlic, chopped
1 chicken, cut into quarters
Salt and freshly ground pepper
to taste
Chicken broth to cover
(6 to 8 cups)
2 bay leaves
1 tablespoon dried Mexican
oregano, crumbled

Serves 4

There's a big covered market right in the center of Oaxaca, and all the side streets around the market are filled with open-air food stalls where you can get fabulous things like grilled corn on the cob, all kinds of tortilla dishes, and grilled chicken like this—marinated and braised before being browned over charcoal.

In a glass baking dish, combine the lemon juice, 4 tablespoons of the olive oil, and the garlic. Add the chicken to the dish and turn it, rubbing the marinade all over. Sprinkle with salt and pepper. Cover and refrigerate for 3 to 4 hours.

Remove the chicken from the refrigerator 30 minutes before cooking. Drain the chicken. In a Dutch oven or flameproof casserole over medium heat, heat 2 tablespoons of the remaining oil and cook the chicken until lightly browned all over. Add the chicken broth, bay leaves, and oregano. Bring to a simmer, cover, and cook for 30 minutes, or until tender. Remove from the heat and let chicken sit in the broth until cool to the touch.

Light a fire in a charcoal grill or preheat a gas grill or a broiler. Drain the chicken, pat it dry with paper towels, and coat it with the remaining 2 tablespoons olive oil. Grill or broil the chicken for about 10 minutes on each side, or until well browned.

SOME OF THE MOST DOWN-HOME FOOD in the world is cooked right on the street and sold from stands by one-person operations. In Oaxaca, the women use open charcoal stoves on folding stands. All the women wear gingham aprons embroidered with flowers, and they make wonderful dishes like squash blossom empanadas and tortillas cooked in black mole sauce. These are the tastes of home for the many different Indian peoples in the state of Oaxaca.

Junkanoo Chicken

3 pounds chicken wings
    Salt and freshly ground black
        pepper to taste
    Cayenne pepper to taste
1 tablespoon dried thyme,
    crumbled
1 tablespoon dry mustard
1 tablespoon ground ginger
    About 2 tablespoons freshly
        squeezed lime juice

Serves 6 to 8

Junkanoo is the Bahamas' Carnival. It's big fun. Bands and costumes, masks and dancers in the streets. Junkanoo is said to have West African roots. Legend has it that the tradition began in the 1800s when an enslaved king named John Canoe demanded that his people be allowed to celebrate together once a year. His slave masters agreed, and the dancing began and it still hasn't stopped. Junkanoo is a major party, and what's a party without some chicken wings?

Sprinkle the chicken with salt, black pepper, and cayenne pepper. Make a paste of the remaining ingredients and coat the chicken. Place the chicken in a glass baking dish. Cover and refrigerate overnight.

Remove from the refrigerator 30 minutes before cooking. Preheat the oven to 350°. Bake the chicken for 35 to 40 minutes, or until brown and crisp.

WHEN YOU SHOP FOR CHICKEN IN A supermarket, make sure to check the sell-by date. That date is 7 to 10 days after the chicken was slaughtered, and it's the last day the chicken can be sold.

And make sure you keep the area you prepare the chicken in clean because we don't want to worry about salmonella.

Zuni Green Chili Stew

3 poblano chilies
1 pound cubed lamb stew meat
2 tablespoons all-purpose flour
2 tablespoons corn oil
1/4 teaspoon freshly ground black
     pepper
2 yellow onions, chopped
3 (14-ounce) cans hominy, rinsed
     and drained
1 small dried red pepper,
     crushed
1 tablespoon salt
2 cloves garlic, crushed
2 teaspoons minced fresh
     oregano
1/2 cup minced fresh parsley
4 cups chicken broth

Serves 6 to 8

The Spanish brought sheep to what is now the American Southwest. Today, the Navajo and Zuni Indians raise sheep on the plains of New Mexico. This Zuni version of lamb stew is made with poblano chilies and hominy. It's great with Black Pepper Corn Bread (page 62).

Oven an open flame of a stove burner, or under a preheated broiler, roast the chilies, turning as necessary. Place in a paper bag, close the bag, and let the chilies steam for 15 minutes. Peel off the skins and set aside. Dust the lamb cubes with the flour.

In a large, heavy skillet over medium heat, heat the oil and brown the meat on all sides. Add the black pepper. Using a slotted spoon, transfer the meat to paper towels or brown paper bags to drain. Add the onions to the pan and sauté until golden brown, about 8 minutes. Return the meat to the skillet. Add all the remaining ingredients, cover, and simmer, stirring occasionally, for 2 hours, or until the meat is tender.

Zuni Green Chili Stew

Maryland Fried Chicken au Grand Duc

1 (3-pound) chicken, cut into
    serving pieces
    Salt and freshly ground pepper
    to taste
    Garlic powder to taste
1 teaspoon dried marjoram
1 cup all-purpose flour
    Peanut oil, for deep-frying
1 cup half-and-half

    Serves 4

In his book *The Big Sea*, Langston Hughes writes about working in Paris in a Montmartre nightclub called Le Grand Duc, where Florence, a diva from Harlem, was the star. That inspired me to make this dish.

Sprinkle the chicken with salt, pepper, and garlic powder. Combine the marjoram and flour and place in a large paper bag. Add the chicken to the bag, close the bag, and shake until the chicken is thoroughly coated. Remove and reserve 2 tablespoons of the seasoned flour.

In a large cast-iron skillet over medium heat, heat 1 inch of peanut oil until almost smoking. Add the chicken and fry until well browned, turning frequently with tongs. Transfer the chicken to paper towels to drain. Pour off all but 1 or 2 tablespoons of the oil. Add the reserved flour to the oil and stir over medium heat, stirring for 1 or 2 minutes until the flour turns a light brown. Gradually stir in the half-and-half. Reduce the heat to low and cook on low, stirring constantly, until thickened. Pour into a gravy boat and serve alongside the chicken, or serve the chicken with the sauce poured over it.

NOW, IN THE BIG SEA, THERE WAS A fellow named Bruce, described by Langston as an enormous brown skin with one eye. He was the cook. Florence might have been the singing star, but Bruce was the kitchen star. Nobody, but nobody, except his helper, Langston, was allowed in the kitchen. A waiter once dared to set foot in Bruce's domain. For having broken the rules, he had a pan of pancake batter flung over his head. Langston didn't say where Bruce was from, but his specialties were corn fritters with gravy, Boston baked beans, and Maryland fried chicken. If you want to find out more about what went on in Le Grand Duc and in Montmartre, called "Harlem on the Seine" in the twenties, read The Big Sea.

Chicken Souse

1 chicken, cut up

1/2 cup freshly squeezed lemon
juice

Salt and freshly ground pepper
to taste

Minced Scotch bonnet chili
to taste

2 onions, chopped

2 stalks celery, chopped

6 whole allspice berries

1 bay leaf

1 teaspoon dried thyme

1 small green or red bell pepper,
seeded, deribbed, and
chopped

Serves 4

This Bahamian stew is quite tangy because of the lemon. It's very flavorful and reminiscent of a chicken dish that the Senegalese make. Some people might find it an acquired taste because it's so tart. It's very good with hot grits or rice, or you can eat it at room temperature.

Place the chicken in a pot and bathe it with the lemon juice. Sprinkle with salt, pepper, and chili. Add water to cover. Bring to a boil, reduce the heat to a simmer, and add all the remaining ingredients. Cover and cook for 30 to 40 minutes, or until tender. Taste and adjust the seasonings. Remove and discard the bay leaf. Serve the chicken immediately, or let cool to room temperature.

HAVE YOU HEARD OF CHICKENS COMING home to roost? Know where that came from? Well, according to one of Aesop's fables, it seems there was a bee who begged the god Jupiter for a stinger to hurt people who came after the bee's honey. That's understandable. Jupiter granted her wish, but the honey bee paid a dear price. Whenever she stung anyone, she would die. See, the bee wished harm on others, then harm came to her. The moral of Aesop's fable? Evil wishes, like chickens, come home to roost.

Ticket-to-Paradise Chicken

1 chicken, cut into serving
   pieces
Salt and freshly ground black
   pepper to taste
Cayenne pepper to taste
1/4 cup freshly squeezed lime
   juice
2 tablespoons vegetable oil
2 tablespoons dark rum
1/2 cup raisins
2 tomatoes, peeled and chopped
2 tablespoons minced fresh
   parsley
Paprika to taste
1/2 pineapple, peeled, cored, and
   cubed
1 cup fresh bread crumbs
2 tablespoons unsalted butter
Saffron Rice, for serving
   (page 29)
Cilantro sprigs, for garnish

Serves 4

The pots are always cooking in the Bahamas, from Bimini, the island that enchanted Adam Clayton Powell Jr. and Ernest Hemingway; to Cat Island, where Sidney Poitier was born; to San Salvador, the first landing place of Columbus; to Eleuthera, where they claim to grow the juiciest pineapple this side of heaven. But even if your pineapple doesn't come from Eleuthera, this Bahamian dish is still a ticket to paradise.

Sprinkle the chicken with salt, black pepper, and cayenne pepper. Place in a glass baking dish and pour the lime juice over the chicken. Cover and refrigerate for 2 or 3 hours.

Take the chicken out of the refrigerator 30 minutes before cooking. Drain the chicken and pat dry with paper towels. In a large skillet over medium heat, heat the oil and quickly brown the chicken on all sides. Add the rum, raisins, tomatoes, parsley, and paprika. Reduce the heat to low, cover, and cook for 25 to 35 minutes, or until tender. Taste and adjust the seasonings. Set aside and keep warm.

Coat the pineapple in the bread crumbs. In a skillet, melt the butter over medium heat and sauté the pineapple cubes until golden brown. Serve the chicken on a bed of Saffron Rice and pour the pan sauce over the chicken. Garnish with the pineapple cubes and cilantro.

THE BAHAMAS ARE OUR CAROLINA cousins because, before the Revolutionary War, these islands were part of the Carolinas. With soothing tropical warmth, miles of colorful beachfront architecture, and cities that hum to the rhythm of a rich history, the Bahamas make up a country that must be felt, seen, heard, and tasted.

Roast Chicken with Banana Stuffing

1 (4- to 5-pound) roasting
   chicken
   Juice of 2 limes

Banana Stuffing

3 cups cooked white long-grain
   rice
3 ripe bananas, peeled and
   chopped
2 tablespoons golden raisins
1 teaspoon grated fresh ginger
1/2 teaspoon freshly grated
   nutmeg
   Salt to taste

2 tablespoons honey
1 cup freshly squeezed orange
   juice
   Salt and freshly ground pepper
   to taste
2 tablespoons dark rum
   (optional)

Serves 4 to 6

When I first heard of this Haitian dish, I didn't think I'd like it. The idea of roast chicken with bananas, rice, raisins, orange juice, and honey seemed odd to me. Now, I don't usually like to use the word *exotic* with regard to food, but this is an exotic dish. It's wonderful! And it's not too sweet. The honey is used to make a glaze for the chicken. If you want to impress somebody, make this dish, and use a free-range chicken. They really do have more flavor.

Preheat the oven to 350°. Bathe the chicken in the lime juice inside and out and set aside. To make the stuffing: In a large bowl, combine all the ingredients. Place the stuffing in a roasting pan, making a depression in the center, and place the chicken in the center, breast side up. Mix the honey and orange juice until the honey dissolves and pour over the chicken. Sprinkle the chicken with salt and pepper. Roast the chicken, basting occasionally with the pan juices, for 15 to 20 minutes per pound, or until the juices run clear when a knife is inserted in the thickest part of the thigh. Remove from the oven.

If you would like to flambé the chicken: In a small pan, heat the rum and pour over the chicken. Using a long-handled match, light the brandy and flambé the chicken. Serve when the flames subside. Carve the chicken at the table.

ALMOST HALF A MILLION AFRICAN SLAVES won their freedom when Haiti achieved independence in 1804. Almost all Haitians today are their descendents, except for a very small percentage of mulattos and whites.

Roast Chicken with Sage-Apple Corn Bread Dressing

1 (4- to 5-pound) roasting
   chicken
   Juice of 1 lemon
3 tablespoons unsalted butter at
   room temperature
   Salt and freshly ground pepper
   to taste
1 small onion, halved
1 stalk celery

Sage-Apple Corn Bread Dressing

1 pound pork sausage
2 tart apples, peeled, cored, and
   chopped
4 cups crumbled Skillet Corn
   Bread (page 63)
4 tablespoons unsalted butter
2 stalks celery, chopped
1 large onion, chopped
1/4 cup minced fresh sage
1 teaspoon dried thyme,
   crumbled
1 teaspoon Bell's poultry
   seasoning
   About 1 cup chicken broth

   About 1/2 cup red or white
   wine, or dry sherry

   Serves 4 to 6

One of the simplest and most satisfying ways to fix chicken is to roast it. Roasters are older and larger than broilers and fryers. Roast chicken and stuffing, or dressing, as we called it, is a classic dish. The dressing is baked separately.

You may use Rock Cornish game hens, one per person, if you wish. They can be roasted or broiled. Season with garlic powder and herbs of your choice under the skin. Rub butter on the skin and bake for 10 minutes at 450°, then about 45 minutes at 350°.

Preheat the oven to 450°. Bathe the chicken in the lemon juice inside and out. Pat the chicken dry with paper towels and rub the butter all over. Sprinkle with salt and pepper inside and out. Place the onion and celery in the body cavity and place the chicken, breast side up, in a roasting pan. Roast for about 10 minutes, then reduce the oven temperature to 350°. Roast the chicken, basting occasionally with the pan juices, for 15 to 20 minutes per pound, or until the juices run clear when a knife is inserted in the thickest part of the thigh.

To make the dressing: In a large skillet, sauté the sausage meat, breaking it up with a spoon. Drain off the excess grease and place the meat in a large bowl. Add the apples and crumbled corn bread. In the same skillet, melt 2 tablespoons of the butter. Add the celery and onion and sauté for 4 or 5 minutes. Add the contents of the skillet to the corn bread mixture.

Melt the remaining 2 tablespoons butter and add to the bowl along with the sage, thyme, and poultry seasoning. Stir and toss with a fork to mix well. Gradually stir in the broth. Place the dressing in a baking dish and bake in the oven along with the chicken for 20 to 30 minutes, or until browned.

When the chicken is done, transfer to a plate and cover loosely with aluminum foil. Spoon off the fat from the roasting pan. Add the wine of your choice to the drippings in the pan and stir over medium heat to scrape up the browned bits from the bottom of the pan. Serve the chicken with the pan juices alongside.

Pipián Verde con Pollo

(Chicken in Green Pumpkin Seed Sauce)

1 stewing chicken
1 onion, halved
1 stalk celery, chopped
1 carrot, peeled and chopped
  Salt and freshly ground pepper
    to taste

Pipián Verde

10 tomatillos, husked, rinsed, and
    quartered
3 jalapeños or green serrano
    chilies, quartered
2 cups chicken broth
2 tablespoons corn oil
1 cup hulled pumpkin seeds,
    lightly toasted and ground to
    a fine powder in a blender
  Salt and freshly ground pepper
    to taste
1 bunch radish leaves
2 large romaine lettuce leaves
2 sprigs cilantro, plus more
    sprigs for garnish

Serves 4 to 6

I would say that Mexican cuisine is one of the top three in the world—the creative spicing and diverse cooking style create recipes that are world class. Though there are eleven main moles, or mother sauces, that all the others spring from, there are as many actual mole combinations as there are Mexican cooks. Each family believes their special way of making mole has to be the best. It is a matter of Mexican pride.

This festive dish from internationally known chef and author Dudley Nieto is chicken in *pipián,* which Dudley explained is a mole flavored with seeds, a dish dating back to pre-Hispanic times. The pumpkin seeds and tomatillos give the sauce its green color, and the pumpkin seeds also help to thicken it. This dish is often served for special occasions.

Place the chicken, onion, celery, carrot, salt, and pepper in a large pot and add water to cover the chicken. Bring to a simmer, cover, and cook for about 45 minutes, or until tender, skimming the foam occasionally. Remove from the heat and let the chicken cool in its stock. Cut the chicken into serving pieces.

In a blender or food processor, purée the tomatillos and chilies with half of the broth until smooth. In a large, heavy saucepan over medium heat, heat the oil and add the purée. Cook for 15 minutes, stirring occasionally. Stir in the remaining broth. Gradually stir in the ground pumpkin seeds, stirring in one direction to prevent the sauce from breaking up. Season with salt and pepper. Simmer for 20 to 25 minutes, or until you see small drops of oil from the pumpkin seeds on the surface.

In a blender or food processor, blend the radish leaves, lettuce, and 2 sprigs cilantro with a little of the pumpkin seed mixture. Return to the pan, stir well, and simmer for 15 minutes. Taste and adjust the seasonings. Serve the chicken in shallow bowls, with a good amount of the sauce poured over. Garnish with cilantro sprigs.

In olden times, pumpkin seeds were ground in a long trough made of volcanic rock called a *metate*. You put the seeds in the *metate* and ground them with a stone roller. It's a lot easier today, when you can use a blender or food processor, like Dudley did. In Mexico, you can buy the pumpkin seeds already ground.

Chicken Stew

1   tablespoon unsalted butter

1   tablespoon olive oil

1   chicken, cut up

1   large onion, chopped

6   cloves garlic, chopped

4   yellow bell peppers, seeded,
     deribbed, and sliced

1   can güero chilies or pickled
     jalapeños, drained and half
     of them sliced in half

4   tomatoes, chopped

2   pounds small potatoes, peeled
     and cut into 1-inch diagonal
     slices

2   pounds carrots, peeled and
     cut into 1-inch diagonal
     slices

2   pounds green plantains,
     peeled and cut into 1-inch
     diagonal slices

2   bay leaves
     Salt and freshly ground black
     pepper to taste
     Cayenne pepper to taste

3   cups chicken broth

Serves 4 to 6

There was a time when there was a chicken in every yard. That's how Charlie "Yardbird" Parker got his name—he loved chicken. This stew is a variation on a dish I had at Maria Ortega's house in Mexico City. It is an Afro-Mexican dish from the west coast of Mexico near Acapulco. Serve it with rice.

In a large skillet or Dutch oven over medium heat, melt the butter with the olive oil and sauté the chicken until browned on both sides. Transfer the chicken to a plate. Add the onion and garlic to the pan and sauté until lightly browned. Add the bell peppers, chilies, tomatoes, potatoes, carrots, plantains, bay leaves, and seasonings. Return the chicken to the pan, placing it on top of the mixture. Add the broth. Cover and simmer until the chicken is tender, about 40 minutes. Remove and discard the bay leaves before serving.

Picnic Chicken

1¹/2 cups buttermilk

1 frying chicken, cut into serving
  pieces

1 cup all-purpose flour

  Salt and freshly ground pepper
    to taste

  Garlic powder to taste

  Paprika to taste

  Vegetable or peanut oil for
    frying

Serves 4

To me, a picnic is the marriage of potato salad and fried chicken.
So here's the dish to take along on your next picnic. In this recipe,
I'm using vegetable oil for frying, but I feel obligated to tell you that
for real fried chicken, the real McCoy, you need a black cast-iron
skillet and lard.

Pour the buttermilk into a glass bowl. Add the chicken pieces, cover,
and refrigerate for at least 3 hours. Remove the chicken from the
refrigerator about 30 minutes before frying.

In a heavy paper bag, combine the flour, salt, pepper, garlic powder,
and paprika. In a colander, drain the chicken and shake to remove the
excess buttermilk. Place the chicken pieces in the paper bag, close
the bag, and shake well to coat all the chicken pieces evenly with the
seasoned flour.

Pour at least 1¹/2 inches of oil into a large, heavy skillet and heat the
oil until fragrant. Add the chicken pieces and cook, turning several
times, until golden brown, about 15 minutes. Transfer to paper towels
or brown paper bags to drain.

*WHEN I USED TO GO TO AND FROM HOME
to South Carolina, we took our shoebox
packed with fried chicken, white bread,
and pound cake. You can laugh about
the white bread all you want, but that
white bread caked with golden crusted
chicken skin and pound cake crumbs
was heavenly. That was good eating.*

Cachupa

2 cups dried corn

1/4 cup dried red kidney beans

4 quarts chicken broth or water

2 bay leaves

6 tablespoons olive oil

1 pound lean salt pork, chopped

2 onions, chopped

6 cloves garlic, chopped, or
   more to taste

2 tomatoes, seeded and
   chopped

8 ounces chorizo sausage or
   garlic sausage, sliced

1 small cabbage, cored and cut
   into quarters

   Salt and freshly ground pepper
   to taste

   Piri-piri sauce, for serving

Serves 8 to 10

Cachupa is the national dish of the Cape Verde Islands. It is very old: a hearty, stick-to-your-bones stew that is a staple in every Cape Verdean home. Depending on which island you're from, the ingredients might change a bit. They tell me that on Cape Verde, a pot of this stew is like a crystal ball: If it's been a good year, the stew will have plenty of vegetables; in a drought year, few. A family of means might have pork, chicken, beef, and even tuna in their stew. No matter, this stew is one where the ingredients marry, and it's good.

Pick over and rinse the corn and beans. Soak separately overnight in water to cover. Place the corn in a large stockpot and add the broth or water. Bring to a boil and cook for 10 minutes. Spoon off and discard the froth that collects on the top. Add the beans, 1 of the bay leaves, and 2 tablespoons of the olive oil. Bring to a boil. Reduce heat to a steady simmer, cover, and cook for 1 hour. Add the salt pork. Cover and cook for an additional 1 1/2 hours, or until the beans and corn are tender. Throughout cooking, make sure that liquid covers the corn and beans.

In a skillet over medium heat, heat the remaining 4 tablespoons oil and sauté the onions, garlic, and tomatoes until the onions are tender, about 5 minutes. Add the remaining bay leaf. Add the mixture to the stockpot. Add the sausage, cabbage, salt, and pepper.

Remove the cachupa from the heat and let stand for at least 20 minutes. The spices and salt will be absorbed into the corn and beans, and the "gravy" will take on a special texture. Remove and discard the bay leaves. Arrange the meats and vegetables on a large platter and serve the corn and beans from a bowl. Serve piri-piri sauce for those who want it.

PIRI-PIRI IS AN AFRICAN WORD FOR HOT pepper, so piri-piri sauce just means any hot pepper sauce, like Tabasco or one of the many others. The Creole culture of the Cape Verde Islands and the Cape Verdean–American community is rooted in the Middle Passage and West Africa and Portugal.

Pozole

1 (14-ounce) can hominy, rinsed
   and drained
8 ounces pork shoulder, chopped
2 cups chicken broth
1 white onion, chopped
6 cloves garlic, minced
2 tablespoons chili powder
1 tablespoon dried Mexican
   oregano
1 teaspoon dried mint
1 tablespoon red pepper flakes
2 teaspoons ground cumin
3 quarts water
   Salt to taste
   Lime wedges, for serving

Serves 4 to 6

Pozole is the Mexican word for hominy, and it also means a stew made with hominy and corn. In Mexico, they make their own hominy by processing dried white field corn kernels in a lime solution to remove the hulls. *Pozole* is a holiday dish! In New Mexico, they eat *pozole* on New Year's Day for good luck all year long (but they spell it *posole*). I first had this when I attended a feast of joy in Santa Clara Pueblo. So along with Hoppin' John, the Southern dish of rice and black-eyed peas eaten for good luck, I have a bowl of *pozole.*

In a large pot, combine all the ingredients except the lime wedges. Bring to a boil, reduce the heat to low, and simmer, uncovered, until the meat is tender and the broth is flavorful, 3 to 5 hours. Add water as needed to keep the hominy and meat covered. The finished stew will have the consistency of a thick soup. Spoon off as much fat as possible. Taste and adjust the seasonings and serve with lime wedges.

TO FULLY APPRECIATE THE DIVERSE Mexican cuisine, we must first understand this country's unique history. Mexico's people, like its food, are an eclectic mixture of Spanish, French, Indian, and African heritages, all coming together to produce a tasty creole blend.

Manchamanteles

2 pounds country-style pork ribs

1 bay leaf

1/2 teaspoon dried thyme, crumbled

1/2 teaspoon ground cumin

1/2 teaspoon dried Mexican oregano, crumbled

Sauce

2 ancho chilies

1 large onion, chopped

3 tomatoes, peeled and chopped

4 tablespoons olive oil or corn oil

2 bay leaves

1 teaspoon ground cumin

1 teaspoon dried Mexican oregano, crumbled

2 tablespoons packed brown sugar

Salt and freshly ground pepper to taste

2 cups reserved pork stock from the pork ribs (above)

2 green plantains, peeled and sliced

1 cup chopped fresh pineapple

2 Granny Smith apples, peeled, cored, and quartered

2 pears, peeled, cored, and quartered

1 cup distilled white vinegar

Cilantro sprigs, for garnish

Serves 4 to 6

This is a simplified version of a complex and wonderful dish I had in Mexico, known as "tablecloth stainer" because it's so mouth-wateringly good that you're bound to stain the table with the dark red sauce.

Place the ribs, bay leaf, thyme, cumin, and oregano in a pot and add water to cover. Bring to a boil, reduce the heat to low, cover, and simmer until tender, about 1 1/2 hours. Drain the ribs and reserve 2 cups of the stock. Spoon as much fat as possible from the surface of the stock.

Meanwhile, to make the sauce: Soak the chilies in hot water to cover for 1 hour; drain, reserving the soaking liquid. In a blender or food processor, process the drained chilies, onion, and tomatoes with a little of the reserved soaking liquid to make a smooth purée.

In a large, heavy saucepan over medium-high heat, heat 3 table-spoons of the oil and add the purée. Cook, stirring constantly, for 2 to 3 minutes. Add the bay leaves, cumin, oregano, brown sugar, salt, and pepper. Cook, stirring occasionally, for about 10 minutes. Stir in the reserved pork stock.

In another saucepan over medium heat, heat the remaining 1 table-spoon oil and sauté the fruit for 2 or 3 minutes, stirring constantly. Add the sautéed fruit and the vinegar to the ribs. Pour the chili mixture over the fruit, reduce the heat to low, cover, and cook for 30 minutes. Remove and discard the bay leaves. Serve the stew in deep plates, garnished with cilantro.

PIGS WERE BROUGHT TO THE AMERICAS on Columbus's first trip in 1492. Easy to raise, fertile, possessing a succulent meat that could be utilized in so many ways, they were quickly adopted by the Native Americans as a new source of animal protein.

Cuban Whole Roast Pig

1 (40- to 45-pound) pig
Several bottles La Lechonera
marinade (made with sour
orange juice, available in
Spanish stores)

Paste
2 bunches cilantro, stemmed
2 bunches flat-leaf parsley,
stemmed
Cloves from 1 head garlic
3 tablespoons corn oil
1/2 cup water
11/2 onions, chopped
1/2 cup black peppercorns, ground
1 container Spanish seasoning
salt (available in Spanish
stores)
1 container dried oregano

Serves 45 to 50

Across the Americas, pork has been adapted to local cultures and affected by the special techniques people brought here from far-away places. In Cuba, for example, pork has been the most popular meat for years. Most special occasions are highlighted by a whole roast pig. Here is chef Larry Tucker's recipe for whole suckling pig cooked in a smoke-roaster known as a China box, the way it's done in Cuba.

Pour the marinade over the pig and marinate for 16 to 18 hours in a China box or other closed container large enough to hold the pig.

To make the paste: In a blender or food processor, combine the cilantro, parsley, garlic, oil, water, and onions and purée until smooth. Pour into a bowl and stir in the pepper, salt, and oregano.

Light a charcoal fire in a smoker, a barrel grill with a cover, or a China box. Let the coals cook down to low. With a large, sharp knife, make deep slits all over the skin of the pig. Using a tablespoon, stuff the paste into the slits, leaving a little to spread all over the pig. Slow-roast the pig on one side, covered, for 3 hours, then turn, cover, and roast another 3 hours, replenishing the coals as needed.

THE BOX LARRY USED TO ROAST THE PIG is an insulated rectangular smoke-roaster called a China box. The pig or other food is placed on a rack in the bottom of the smoke-roaster, and lighted charcoal is placed on a grate at the top of the box, so that the heat radiates down. For information on ordering a China box, see page 154.

Pork Tenderloin with George Washington Carver Peanut Sauce

1/2 cup soy sauce
 4 cloves garlic, minced
 1 small onion, finely chopped
1/2 teaspoon cayenne pepper
 1 teaspoon ground coriander
 2 tablespoons white wine
    vinegar
 2 tablespoons water
 2 pork tenderloins, about 12
    ounces each
 2 bacon slices

Peanut Sauce
 1 cup milk
1/4 cup chunky peanut butter
 1 onion, finely chopped
1/4 cup soy sauce
    Red pepper flakes to taste

Serves 6 to 8

You know the expression "high on the hog." Pork tenderloin is a good example. True to its name, the tenderloin is the most tender part of the pig, and when it comes to calories, total fat, and cholesterol, pork tenderloin measures up to baked chicken breast. There are interesting ways to fix pork tenderloin. One of my favorites is tenderloin roast with a peanut sauce I named after George Washington Carver, the former slave who became a famous botanist by developing hundreds of uses for the peanut and other plants. The bacon in this recipe adds the fat needed. So, you might say that this dish is high and low on the hog. It's great with Sweet Potato–Corn Muffins (page 61) and a side of collard greens.

In a glass baking dish, combine the soy sauce, garlic, onion, cayenne pepper, coriander, vinegar, and water. Stir to blend. Add the tenderloins and turn to coat them on all sides. Cover and refrigerate for at least 8 hours, turning occasionally. Remove the tenderloins from the refrigerator at least 30 minutes before baking. Transfer the tenderloins to a shallow roasting pan, reserving the marinade. Place 1 bacon slice on top of each tenderloin.

Preheat the oven to 325°. In a small saucepan, boil the reserved marinade for at least 5 minutes, then set aside. Roast the tenderloins uncovered, basting often with the marinade, for about 1 hour, or until a meat thermometer inserted in the thickest part of the meat reads 160°.

While the pork is roasting, make the peanut sauce: In a blender, combine all the sauce ingredients and pulse until smooth. Place in a small saucepan and cook over low heat, stirring frequently, for about 5 minutes, or until the sauce is heated thoroughly, adding more liquid if it is too thick. Set aside and keep warm.

Place the roasted pork on a platter, cover loosely with aluminum foil, and let stand for 10 minutes; then slice and serve with the warm peanut sauce.

Peggy's Company Pork Pie

1 pound ground pork
1 large onion, chopped
  Chili powder to taste
  Salt and freshly ground
    pepper to taste
1 (14-ounce) can chopped
    tomatoes with their liquid
2 tablespoons tomato paste
1 tablespoon chili powder, or to
    taste
1/2 cup raisins
1/2 cup shredded Cheddar cheese
1/2 recipe Skillet Corn Bread
    batter (page 63), made with
    yellow cornmeal

Serves 6

A woman I used to know named Peggy made this dish. People told her how good it was, so after a while it was the only dish she made for company. This is a quick supper or lunch dish. Ground pork, for me, is much more flavorful than ground beef.

In a large skillet, brown the meat over medium heat, stirring frequently. Pour off and discard the excess fat. Add the onion and cook for about 3 minutes. Stir in the chili powder, salt, and pepper. Stir in the tomatoes, tomato paste, and raisins. Bring to a simmer, reduce the heat to low, and cook for 30 minutes.

Preheat the oven to 350°. Blend the cheese into the pork mixture. Pour into a greased 2-quart casserole. Spoon the corn bread batter on top of the meat mixture to cover evenly. Bake for about 35 minutes, or until the topping is golden brown.

YOU'VE HEARD OF A PIG IN A POKE. IT seems that in the 1600s, English merchants had a trick they used to play on people buying pigs. Piglets were sold in a little sack, called a poke. However, when some people got home they found that the tricky merchant had put a cat in the poke instead of a piglet. When the unsuspecting buyer got home and opened the poke, he let the cat out of the bag—that's where that phrase came from. And that's why we're warned never to buy a pig in a poke.

Moletes de Tinga Poblana
(Shredded Pork with Mexican Sausage)

Tinga Poblana

1¹/2 pounds pork shoulder, chopped
    Pinch of salt
  6 ounces Mexican chorizo
      sausage, removed from
      casings and crumbled
¹/2 small onion, sliced
  3 cloves garlic, minced
¹/4 teaspoon dried thyme,
      crumbled
¹/4 teaspoon dried oregano,
      crumbled
  2 bay leaves
  2 tomatoes, sliced
  1 tablespoon packed brown
      sugar
¹/2 can chipotle chilies in adobo
      sauce, drained (sauce
      reserved) and chopped
    Salt and freshly ground pepper
      to taste

Tortillas

  8 ounces prepared fresh corn
      masa
¹/2 cup flour
  1 cup crumbled queso fresco or
      farmer's cheese
¹/2 teaspoon kosher or sea salt
  1 cup vegetable oil, for deep-
      frying
    Lettuce leaves, for serving
    Cilantro sprigs, for garnish

Makes 12 moletes; serves 6

Chef Dudley Nieto showed me how to make these little turnovers, or *moletes.* You need a tortilla press and prepared masa, available at some Latino markets, to make the tortillas for the *moletes.* The *tinga* is a sweet/sour spicy stuffing for the *moletes,* which are deep-fried and served right away.

Place the meat in a heavy, flameproof casserole and add the pinch of salt and water to cover. Bring to a boil, then reduce the heat to a simmer, cover, and cook until tender, about 40 minutes, adding water to cover as needed. Remove from the heat and let the meat cool to the touch in the stock. Drain the meat, reserving the stock. With your fingers, shred the meat finely.

In a skillet over low heat, cook the sausage, stirring frequently, until the fat is rendered. Add the onion and garlic and sauté for 5 minutes. Add the thyme, oregano, bay leaves, tomatoes, and brown sugar. Simmer for 5 minutes. Add the shredded pork, chipotles, and reserved adobo sauce and simmer for 10 to 15 minutes. Season with salt and pepper. Cover and refrigerate while making the tortillas. Remove the bay leaves before using.

In a bowl, combine the masa, flour, cheese, and salt and mix until smooth. Line each plate of a tortilla press with a circle of waxed paper. Place a ball of about ¹/4 cup masa mixture in the center of the press and close it firmly. Peel the paper off the tortilla. Fill the tortilla with about 1 tablespoon tinga. Press the edges closed. Repeat to use all the masa mixture and tinga.

In a large cast-iron skillet or a Dutch oven, heat the vegetable oil to 375° and cook a few of the moletes until crisp, 3 to 5 minutes; don't add too many to the pan at once or this will lower the temperature of the oil. Using a slotted spoon or a wire-mesh skimmer, transfer to paper towels to drain. Repeat to cook the remaining moletes. Serve at once on lettuce leaves, garnished with cilantro.

Griot

2 pounds pork shoulder, cut into
1-inch cubes

1¹/2 cups freshly squeezed lime
juice

1 large onion, finely chopped

¹/2 cup minced shallots

6 allspice berries

1 tablespoon dried thyme

¹/2 cup freshly squeezed orange
juice

2 Scotch bonnet chilies, minced
Salt and freshly ground pepper
to taste

1 cup vegetable oil, for frying

Serves 8

This is a very popular dish in Haiti; in fact, it's considered the national dish. Gabrielle Loiseau, who is Haitian, showed me how to make this. As it's the favorite dish of the people, *griot* is also served during voodoo ceremonies as an offering to the gods. The West African word *griot* also refers to a male storyteller who traveled from village to village passing along the history of the culture.

Bathe the pork with ¹/2 cup of the lime juice, then drain in a colander. In a bowl, combine the remaining lime juice and all the remaining ingredients except the oil. Add the pork, cover, and refrigerate for at least 3 hours or overnight, turning several times.

Put the pork and its marinade in a large, heavy pot. Bring to a boil. Reduce the heat to low and simmer, uncovered, until the pork is tender but not falling apart, about 1 hour. Drain.

In a large, heavy skillet, heat the oil until almost smoking. Add the pork and cook, turning frequently, until it is crusty and brown on all sides. Using a slotted spoon, transfer to paper towels to drain. Serve at once.

EVEN THOUGH THEY ARE LARGELY Catholic, many Haitian people still practice voodoo rituals that are linked to the African worship of deities. Africans kept their religion during slavery by merging the identities of their deities with those of Catholic saints. Legend has it that voodoo played a role in the Haitian revolution during the 1790s. Boukman Dutty, one of the early leaders, called on the voodoo gods when he planned his revolt. At a secret ceremony, he asked the gods to make his men fearless in battle, and they were. They kicked out the British, the Spanish, and the French.

Troupe Stuffed Pork Chops

6 pork chops, each 3/4 to 1 inch
thick
Sage-Apple Corn Bread
Dressing (page 87), or your
favorite corn bread dressing
Salt and freshly ground pepper
to taste
Garlic powder to taste
1 tablespoon olive oil
About 2 cups chicken broth

Serves 6

In the seventies, when I lived on New York's Upper West Side, my great friend, the great poet Quincy Troupe, was a neighbor. On Broadway there was a wonderful meat store called Oppenheimer's. When our pockets were deep, I would send my daughters to get thick pork chops for stuffing, and every time they would run into Quincy, who asked, "What's your mama cooking tonight?" When he heard stuffed pork chops, he would manage to "visit" at dinnertime. To this day, when anybody says "stuffed pork chops," my family says "Quincy Troupe." So I call these Troupe Stuffed Pork Chops.

Have your butcher cut a large pocket in the side of each chop, or do it yourself with a sharp knife. Preheat the oven to 400°. Fill each chop with 2 or 3 tablespoons of the dressing, taking care not to make them bulge. Sprinkle the chops with salt, pepper, and garlic powder.

In a large skillet over medium-high heat, heat the oil and sear the chops for about 2 minutes on each side. Place the chops in a baking dish and add broth to a depth of about 1/2 inch. Cover with aluminum foil. Place the remaining dressing in another baking dish.

Place the chops in the oven and reduce the oven temperature to 375°. Bake for 30 minutes, then reduce the oven temperature to 350°. Add the baking dish with the dressing to the oven and uncover the pork chops. Bake for another 30 minutes, or until the chops are tender, basting with the broth several times and adding more broth if necessary.

DID YOU KNOW THAT DURING THE WAR of 1812, a New York pork packer, Uncle Sam Wilson, shipped a boatload of several hundred barrels of pork to U.S. troops. It's said that the word on the docks was that "U.S." stood for "Uncle Sam." So the character in the "Uncle Sam Wants You" posters all started with a pork packer in New York.

Okra and Pork in Creole Sauce

1 slice bacon, chopped

2 tablespoons olive oil

1 large onion, chopped

3 cloves garlic, minced

8 ounces ground pork

3 tomatoes, diced

1 small green bell pepper, seeded, deribbed, and chopped

1/2 teaspoon ground cloves

Salt and freshly ground black pepper to taste

Cayenne pepper to taste

1 pound young okra, cut into thin diagonal slices

1 cup chicken broth

Juice of 1 lime

Steamed rice, for serving

Serves 4 to 6

The okra in this dish says that Africa passed through Cuba. Okra is an Old World vegetable in the New World. There's a Cuban proverb that describes this dish perfectly: "The new pleases and the old satisfies." Serve this with rice and plantains.

In a large skillet, cook the bacon until crisp. Transfer the bacon to paper towels to drain. Add the olive oil, onion, and garlic to the same pan and sauté for 3 or 4 minutes. Add the ground pork and cook until the meat is browned. Spoon off the excess fat. Add the tomatoes, bell pepper, cloves, salt, black pepper, and cayenne pepper. Cover and simmer for 30 minutes. Add the okra and stock and simmer for 15 minutes. Stir in the lime juice and bacon. Taste and adjust the seasonings. Serve over rice.

IN ADDITION TO THEIR FOODS AND cooking styles, Africans also brought their rituals and rhythms to Cuba: the mambo, cha cha cha, salsa. Remember Desi Arnaz as Ricky Ricardo in I Love Lucy? *"Babalu!" What you probably didn't know is that when he sang "Babalu," he was singing about making offerings to Babalu-Aye, one of the deities in the Afro-Cuban religion, Santería.*

Food and the celebration of food are very much a part of Cuban life. Though it's not exactly "P.C.," food even flavors the language of courtship. A young woman might refer to her sweetheart as a "piece of bread." Or a good-looking woman might be referred to as a "chicken." Which reminds me of an old Cuban flirtation, "If you cook the way you walk, I'll scrape the pot!"

Grouper and Spinach with Wine Sauce and Plantains

2 cups dry red wine

1/2 cup fish broth or clam juice

2 teaspoons tomato paste

1/4 cup heavy cream

4 (6-ounce) grouper, red snapper, or sea bass fillets

Salt and freshly ground pepper to taste

Flour, for dredging

7 tablespoons olive oil

2 green plantains, peeled and cut into 1/2-inch slices

4 cups packed fresh spinach leaves

2 tablespoons unsalted butter

Serves 4

This recipe from Graycliff in the Bahamas combines tropical ingredients—grouper and green plantains—with a French-inspired wine sauce. It's a sophisticated dish to serve for special occasions.

In a heavy saucepan, cook the red wine over medium heat until it is reduced by half. Add the broth or clam juice and whisk in the tomato paste. Cook again to reduce by about one fourth. Add the cream and cook again to reduce until the sauce begins to thicken. Set aside and keep warm.

Sprinkle the fillets with salt and pepper. Dredge the fillets in flour and shake off the excess. In a large skillet over medium heat, heat 4 tablespoons of the oil and cook the fillets for about 5 minutes on each side, or until golden brown on the outside and opaque throughout on the inside. Transfer to a plate and keep warm.

In a medium skillet over medium heat, heat 2 tablespoons of the oil and sauté the plantains until lightly browned on both sides. Set aside and keep warm.

In a large skillet over medium heat, heat 1 tablespoon of the oil and cook the spinach, stirring constantly, until wilted. Transfer to a colander and press with the back of a spoon to remove some of the liquid.

Quickly divide the spinach among 4 warm plates. Place a fillet on top of each serving of spinach and arrange the plantain slices around the spinach. Stir the butter into the wine sauce until melted. Pour some of the warm wine sauce over each serving and serve at once.

Sautéed Codfish with Onions and Potatoes

8 ounces dried salt cod

4 large boiling potatoes, peeled and chopped

1/4 cup vegetable oil

1 large onion, sliced

Salt and freshly ground pepper to taste

Shredded scallions, for garnish

Serves 4

Almost everyone has a codfish recipe they cook and enjoy. Here's another salt cod recipe from Cape Verde, where this kind of fish is a staple known as *piexe seco.*

Soak the cod in water to cover overnight, changing the water in the morning. Drain and rinse under cold water. Break the fish into chunks and remove all bones. Set aside. Cook the potatoes in salted boiling water until tender, about 15 minutes. Drain and let cool.

In a large saucepan over medium heat, heat the oil and sauté the onion until translucent, about 3 minutes. Add the fish and potatoes and sauté for about 10 minutes, or until the potatoes are lightly browned and crisp but not mushy. Season with salt and pepper. Garnish with scallions and serve.

Curried Codfish

2 teaspoons curry powder

1/2 teaspoon ground saffron

1 teaspoon minced fresh ginger

1 cup fish broth or clam juice

2 fresh codfish, halibut, or sea
    bass fillets, about 12 ounces
    each

2 tablespoons olive oil

1 onion, sliced

3 cloves garlic, minced
    Salt and freshly ground pepper
       to taste
    Cooked rice, for serving

Serves 4

Even before Asians and folks from the Caribbean migrated to Canada, sea captains brought back spices from their travels. This Canadian recipe marries cod, a gift from the Atlantic, and curry. This curry-ginger gravy is perfect for fresh cod. Serve this dish over rice.

Combine the curry powder, saffron, and ginger with a few spoonsful of broth or clam juice to make a paste. Spread the paste over the fillets to coat them evenly. Set aside for 10 minutes.

In a large skillet over medium heat, heat 1 tablespoon of the olive oil and sauté the onion and garlic for about 4 minutes, or until translucent. Push the onion mixture aside and add the remaining 1 tablespoon olive oil to the pan. Add the fish to the pan and sauté for 2 or 3 minutes on each side, or until lightly browned. Add the remaining fish broth or clam juice. Season the fish with salt and pepper. Bring to a simmer, cover, and cook for 10 minutes, or until the fish is opaque throughout. Serve over rice.

CANADA HAS A SPECIAL BOND TO THE African-American community here in the United States. Some Southerners will never forget the debt that is owed to Canada for sheltering our ancestors from the cruelties of slavery. Canada has always been a safe haven for immigrants. Some arrived by boat, some by plane, and others on a very unusual railroad. For African Americans during slavery times, Canada was the freedom stop on the Underground Railroad.

Codfish and Ackee

1/2 pound salt cod with bones

1/2 pound salt cod without bones

1/4 cup olive oil or corn oil

1 large onion, sliced

2 cloves garlic, minced

1 large green bell pepper,
   seeded, deribbed, and
   coarsely chopped

   Minced Scotch bonnet chili
   to taste

3/4 cup tomato sauce

1 (18-ounce) can ackee, rinsed
   and drained

Serves 6

Here's one of Jamaica's most popular dishes, adapted from a recipe in my book *Vibration Cooking.* It's codfish again, this time combined with ackee, a fruit originally from Africa. In Jamaica, ackee is used fresh, of course. It's red and shaped like a pear, though the flesh is a pale yellow. You can find it canned in stores that sell Latin foods. Serve this dish with kidney beans and rice. Using codfish with bones helps to give the special texture of the authentic Jamaican dish.

In a stockpot, soak the codfish in water to cover overnight. Pour off the water and add fresh water to cover. Bring to a boil and cook for 5 minutes. Turn off the heat and let cool to the touch in the water. Drain the fish and remove the bones. Separate the fish into flakes. Set aside.

In a large skillet over medium heat, heat the oil and sauté the onion and garlic until golden. Add the bell pepper and chili and sauté for about 5 minutes. Add the tomato sauce and cook, stirring occasionally, for about 5 minutes. Add the flaked fish, cover, and cook for about 10 minutes. Gently fold in the ackee and cook a few minutes just to heat through.

Codfish Fritters

8 ounces salt cod
2 tablespoons vegetable oil, plus
   oil for frying
2 onions, finely chopped
2 cloves garlic, minced
2 tomatoes, finely chopped
2 scallions, finely chopped
1/2 Scotch bonnet chili, minced
1 1/2 cups all-purpose flour
2 teaspoons baking powder
   About 3/4 cup water

Serves 4

This codfish fritter recipe is from Cape Verde, but similar fritters are also popular in the Caribbean. In Jamaica, they're formed into patties by hand and called "stamp and go." Some claim the name comes from an old sailing term meaning "hurry up." Another common explanation is that it describes how the fritters are made: "stamped" out between the palms, fried briefly, and then eaten on the "go."

Soak the cod in water to cover overnight. Drain and rinse under cold water. Flake the fish and remove all bones. Place the flaked fish in a large bowl.

In a large skillet over medium heat, heat the 2 tablespoons oil and sauté the onions, garlic, tomatoes, scallions, and chili. Stir this mixture into the flaked fish. In a bowl, stir the flour and baking powder together. Add enough water to make a thick batter. Stir this mixture into the flaked fish.

In a large, heavy skillet or Dutch oven over medium heat, heat 1/2 inch of oil until almost smoking. Fry heaping tablespoonsful of batter until golden brown on each side, taking care not to crowd the pan. Using a slotted spoon, transfer to paper towels to drain. Keep warm in a low oven. Repeat to fry the remaning batter. Serve at once.

SALTFISH IS A MAINSTAY OF THE Caribbean. It is variously known as bacalhau (Portuguese), baccalà (Italian), bacalao (Spanish), and salt cod or dried cod (the United States). The salting and drying of foods was introduced to the Caribbean by Africans and Europeans. In the absence of refrigeration, this new method was quickly adopted as a good means of preserving not only fish but also a variety of meats.

Baked Salmon with Corn Sauce

4 (6-ounce) salmon fillets
 Salt and freshly ground pepper
   to taste
 Paprika to taste
1 onion, thinly sliced
4 tablespoons unsalted butter,
   melted
2 tablespoons minced fresh dill

Corn Sauce

2 cups fresh or frozen corn
   kernels
1 tablespoon freshly squeezed
   lemon juice
1 tablespoon white wine vinegar
1/4 cup olive oil
1 jalapeño chili, minced
1 tablespoon chopped fresh
   cilantro
1 tablespoon chopped fresh mint
 Salt and freshly ground pepper
   to taste

 Dill sprigs, for garnish
 Lemon wedges, for serving
   (optional)

 Serves 4

Native Americans in the Northwest fixed salmon in a variety of ways. They smoked it, made chowders out of it, poached it, and baked it on a plank. Here's a dish of baked salmon served with corn sauce. We all know how important corn, or maize, was to Native American culture, and this sauce of corn, peppers, and seasonings accents the taste of the fish. Serve this dish with wild rice.

Preheat the oven to 350°. Place each fillet on a square of aluminum foil, skin side down. Sprinkle with salt, pepper, and paprika. Arrange the onion slices on top of the salmon. Spoon the butter over. Sprinkle with the dill and close up the foil into a packet. Bake for 20 to 25 minutes, or until the salmon is just barely cooked through.

Meanwhile, make the sauce: In a small saucepan, cook the corn, uncovered, in salted boiling water until tender, about 3 minutes. Drain and let cool at room temperature. In a bowl, whisk the lemon juice and vinegar together. Add the remaining ingredients.

Remove the salmon from the foil and place each fillet on a plate. Serve the corn sauce on top of or alongside the salmon. Garnish with dill sprigs and serve with lemon wedges, if desired.

WHEN EUROPEANS ARRIVED IN THIS country in the fifteenth century, there were millions of Native Americans here with impressive skills and technology. There were the spectacular temples and pyramids of the Mayan civilization, and the elaborate cities of the Aztec Empire. And we're still discovering their achievements.

Native Americans have always believed in taking only what they could use from the land, and using whatever they took, and in always giving thanks for the bounty. We can all share in this great lesson as we share in the gifts of life that have been handed down to us by our Native American ancestors.

Salmon Cakes

1 (14-ounce) can red sockeye
    salmon, drained (juice
    reserved) and flaked
1/3 cup cornmeal
2 eggs, beaten
1 tablespoon flour
    Salt and freshly ground pepper
    to taste
    Juice of 1/2 lemon

Serves 6

Salmon cakes, or patties, as some call them, are a great favorite in my house. My mother loved salmon cakes. When she was in her eighties, she was diagnosed with diabetes. The doctor told her she couldn't eat fried foods, and for a woman who loved fried fish and fish cakes, it was bad news. So I made these salmon cakes in the oven for her, and they were just as good as in the skillet. Mama was happy.

Preheat the oven to 350°. Mix all the ingredients together in a bowl and form into 6 patties. If the mixture is too stiff, add some of the reserved salmon juice. Place the patties on a greased baking sheet and bake for 15 to 20 minutes, or until lightly browned.

FISH WAS AN IMPORTANT FOOD SOURCE for many Native Americans. If the buffalo ruled the Great Plains, then in the Northwest, salmon reigned. One old-timer is reported to have said that he saw salmon so thick, you could walk across their backs. The legend is that salmon are not fish at all. They are spirit people who live in a magic village under the sea and are sent upriver in the summer.

Conch Cakes

12 ounces defrosted frozen conch
     meat
1 clove garlic, minced
1 small onion, finely chopped
1/3 cup finely chopped green bell
     pepper
1 shallot, minced
1/2 cup dried bread crumbs
1/2 tablespoon soy sauce
5 drops Tabasco sauce
1/2 tablespoon Dijon mustard
     Salt and freshly ground white
     pepper to taste
1/4 cup heavy cream
2 eggs, lightly beaten
1 tablespoon mayonnaise
1 tablespoon olive oil

Serves 4

Conch cakes, a first cousin to "stamp and go," are the West Indian version of crab cakes. This version is as authentic as you can get because it's from Leonne Reynold of Hotel Villa Creole's kitchen in Port-au-Prince, Haiti. Eat these hot and fresh, along with Leonne's Creamed Corn (page 49).

Place the conch in a heavy plastic bag and pound with a mallet until thin. Place the conch and garlic in a blender or food processor and chop coarsely. Transfer the mixture to a bowl and add the onion, bell pepper, and shallot. Stir in all the remaining ingredients, except the oil, until well mixed.

Shape the mixture into 8 patties. In a large skillet over medium heat, heat the oil and cook half of the patties for about 5 minutes on each side, or until golden brown. Keep warm in a low oven while cooking the remaining patties. Serve at once.

EVERYBODY KNOWS WHAT A CONCH SHELL looks like: It's the one with ruffled edges and a shiny pink inside, and you can use it as a horn or hold it up to your ear to listen to the sea. But not many people eat conch outside of the West Indies, where it provides an abundant sweet meat for soups, chowders, and fried savory cakes. You can find it fresh in Chinese and West Indian markets, but it's much easier to buy it frozen. Pound it with the flat side of a meat pounder to tenderize the tough meat, then shred it.

Huachinango a la Veracruz
(Pan-fried Red Snapper)

2 small (1-pound) red snappers,
  or 4 (6-ounce) snapper fillets
Salt and freshly ground pepper
  to taste
2 tablespoons olive oil
3 to 4 cloves garlic, minced
1 onion, diced
2 tomatoes, diced
2 canned pickled jalapeños,
  drained
10 pimiento-stuffed green olives
1 small bottle capers, drained
1 teaspoon dried oregano,
  crumbled
1 teaspoon dried thyme,
  crumbled
3 bay leaves
1 cup fish broth or chicken
  broth

Serves 4

Veracruz, on the east coast of Mexico, was the port where the Africans, French, and Spanish first landed in a country populated by Native Americans, and Veracruz cuisine shows all these influences. Seafood, of course, is one of the most important ingredients, including the meaty red snapper, abundant off the coast. This is the way to prepare it Veracruz style.

Sprinkle the fish with salt and pepper. In a large skillet over medium heat, heat the oil and cook the fish for 2 or 3 minutes on each side. Add all the remaining ingredients to the pan, sprinkling them over and around the fish. Reduce the heat to low, cover, and cook for 20 to 30 minutes, or until the fish is opaque throughout. Remove and discard the bay leaves. Divide the fish and sauce among 4 warm plates and serve.

IN THE STATE AND CITY OF VERACRUZ, you can see traces of Mexico's African-Creole heritage in the features of some of its citizens, descendants of African slaves brought here by the Spanish. The influence of the Africans can be felt today in Veracruzano culture, food, and music. Some anthropologists, attempting to explain the African features of the giant stone Olmec heads found in Veracruz state, have speculated that the Olmecs, the first great civilization of Mexico, may have had an African origin.

Hurricane Ham Fritters

1 pound defrosted frozen conch
   meat
1/2 cup all-purpose flour
1 teaspoon baking powder
1 egg, slightly beaten
  About 1/2 cup milk
1 clove garlic, minced
1 small onion, finely chopped
  Salt and freshly ground black
   pepper to taste
  Cayenne pepper to taste
  About 2 cups vegetable oil, for
   deep-frying

Serves 4 to 6

What's hurricane ham? Well, other than Nassau, the other 699 islands that make up the Bahamas are known as "the out islands." The story goes that during hurricane season, when folks on the out islands couldn't get to Nassau to purchase other meats, they took conch, flattened and tenderized it, and hung it in the sun to cure it. Hence the name "hurricane ham." This is my variation, which I call Hurricane Ham Fritters.

Place the conch in a heavy plastic bag and pound with a mallet until thin. Finely chop the conch by hand or in a food processor. In a large bowl, combine the flour, baking powder, and egg. Stir in the milk a little at a time to make a fairly stiff batter. Stir in the conch, garlic, onion, salt, pepper, and cayenne.

In a large skillet, heat the oil until hot but not smoking. Drop in the batter by the heaping tablespoonful, but don't crowd them. Fry until golden brown, 1 to 2 minutes on each side. Using a slotted spoon, drain on paper towels. Serve at once. Conch fritters are like pancakes: from the pan to the mouth!

CONCH HAS A TOUGH MEAT THAT HAS to be beaten before it's ready for soups, salads, or as the centerpiece of a fantastic meal. This food was familiar to the West African slaves who were brought to the Bahamas, where conch was and is abundant and easy to harvest. Conch is believed to be an aphrodisiac, and older Bahamians make a special tonic from fresh conch that is said to be rich in vitamins and iron.

Jerked Veggie Burgers

2 cups cooked black beans,
    drained and mashed
4 tablespoons olive oil
1 egg, slightly beaten
3/4 cup fresh bread crumbs
1 onion, diced
2 cloves garlic, minced
1 teaspoon jerk seasoning
1/4 teaspoon salt, or to taste
    Freshly ground pepper to taste
    Vegetable broth as needed

Serves 6

A vegetarian at a burger and hot-dog cookout can really feel like a second-class guest, so this recipe is for them. This is a vegetarian burger that everyone will enjoy. You can eat it on pita bread with lettuce, tomatoes, red onions, and cucumbers, or on a bun with salsa, or in any other variation you want.

In a bowl, combine the beans, 2 tablespoons of the olive oil, the egg, bread crumbs, onion, garlic, jerk seasoning, salt, and pepper. Stir to blend. Add 1 tablespoon of broth at a time if needed to make a thick, scoopable mixture.

In a large skillet over medium heat, heat the remaining 2 tablespoons oil until fragrant. Scoop out one sixth of the mixture for each portion and place in the hot oil. Brown the burgers for about 4 minutes on each side, or until firm and crisp. Serve warm.

MORE AND MORE PEOPLE ARE BECOMING vegetarians. They are our friends and family members. One study reports that 88 percent of the people who became vegetarians did so because of health concerns, but 86 percent of the people in that same poll said they stayed vegetarians because they liked the way the food tasted.

Cecilia's Olive and Cream Cheese Sandwiches

8 ounces cream cheese at room temperature

3/4 cup pimiento-stuffed green olives, finely chopped

Salt and freshly ground black pepper to taste

Milk as needed

About 8 slices white bread, crusts trimmed

Serves 4

In the sixties, I lived in New York City on the Lower East Side. Cooking and eating with my neighbors, I enjoyed the tastes of the world. To paraphrase Ntozake Shange's poem "Where the Mississippi Meets the Amazon," foodwise, for me the Lower East Side was where the Mississippi meets the Mediterranean, the Nile, the Niger, the Adriatic, the Atlantic, and the Caribbean. My Cuban neighbor Cecilia was one cooking woman. She could boil a pot of water, stir it up, and serve it, and it would taste like an exquisite stock. I have dozens of delicious memories of the scrumptious Cuban dinners she fixed, but—would you believe?—my favorite is the little white bread sandwiches with a cream cheese and olive spread.

In a small bowl, combine the cream cheese, olives, salt, and pepper. Stir until blended. Cover and refrigerate for at least 1 hour. Bring to room temperature before spreading on bread. If the mixture is too stiff, add a little milk. Spread the mixture on half of the bread slices and top with the remaining slices. Cut each sandwich into 4 squares or triangles.

There is an old Cuban saying that goes something like this: "The bread of your own home is always good." I like that. For me it sums up what traditional Cuban cooking is all about. Family food. What we call in Carolina, country cooking. And that's true. Wherever you go in Cuba, you find food that comes from the home bringing family and friends together.

Black Mushroom Rice Cakes

2 cups long-grain white rice

4¼ cups water

1½ ounces dried djon djon or
dried shiitake mushrooms

1 tablespoon olive oil

2 tablespoons finely chopped
green bell pepper

4 tablespoons finely chopped
onion

1 clove garlic, minced

1 teaspoon salt

1 carrot, peeled and grated

4 ounces green beans, trimmed
and finely chopped

2 eggs, lightly beaten

½ teaspoon freshly ground white
pepper

1 cup heavy cream

⅓ cup vegetable oil

Serves 8

The only thing better than Haitian rice with black mushrooms is the same rice made into cakes and fried. This dish is from Leonne Reynold of Hotel Villa Creole in Port-au-Prince, Haiti. She uses the local djon djon mushrooms, but dried shiitakes are a great substitute. Serve these rice cakes with roast chicken and Leonne's Creamed Corn (page 49) for a fabulous meal.

Rinse the rice and drain it. In a small saucepan, bring 2¼ cups of the water to a boil. Add the mushrooms and cook for 10 minutes. Drain in a colander set over a bowl. Let the mushrooms cool to the touch, then squeeze all the juice from them through the colander into the bowl. Reserve the juice and let stand for about 5 minutes for the sediment to settle. Carefully pour or measure out 2 cups of the liquid, making sure not to disturb the sediment.

In a medium saucepan over medium heat, heat the olive oil and sauté the bell pepper, 1 tablespoon of the onion, and the garlic for about 3 minutes, or until the onion is translucent. Gradually stir in the reserved mushroom juice, then ½ teaspoon of the salt. Bring to a boil and stir in half of the rice. Reduce the heat to a simmer, cover, and cook for about 20 minutes, or until the rice is tender.

Meanwhile, in another medium saucepan, bring the remaining 2 cups water to a boil. Stir in the remaining rice, the remaining onion, and the remaining ½ teaspoon salt. Reduce the heat to a simmer, cover, and cook for about 20 minutes, or until the rice is tender.

Cook the carrot and green beans in salted boiling water for 2 minutes. Drain. In a large bowl, combine the two rice preparations, the carrot and beans, the eggs, pepper, and cream. Taste and adjust the seasonings.

In a large skillet over medium heat, heat the vegetable oil until fragrant. Form the rice mixture into 8 patties and cook a few at a time for about 3 minutes on each side, or until golden brown. Transfer to a baking sheet and place in a low oven to keep warm. Repeat with the remaining rice mixture. Serve at once.

Spinach on Spinach Pasta

8 ounces spinach linguine or
   fettuccine
2 tablespoons olive oil
1 onion, chopped
3 cloves garlic, minced
1 bunch fresh spinach, washed,
   stemmed, and chopped
   Salt and freshly ground pepper
   to taste
2 small tomatoes, peeled and
   diced
1/3 cup crumbled feta cheese

Serves 4

We all remember our mothers telling us to eat our vegetables. They knew what they were talking about, and so did Popeye. This double dose of spinach is easy and fast and good for you. The important thing is to use the best-tasting tomatoes you can find! I like it with feta best, but Parmesan works too.

In a large pot of salted boiling water, cook the pasta until al dente, about 10 minutes. Meanwhile, in a large skillet over medium heat, heat the oil and sauté the onion for 3 or 4 minutes. Add the garlic and sauté for 1 minute. Add the spinach, salt, and pepper. Cover and cook briefly until the spinach wilts. Add the tomatoes and cook until softened. Drain the pasta and stir in the spinach mixture. Serve at once with the cheese alongside to sprinkle over.

SPINACH, WHICH CAME TO EUROPE during the Middle Ages, has been traced to Asia, where spinach plants were presented to the rulers of the Tang Dynasty of China by the king of Nepal in the seventh century A.D. Today in the States, spinach is celebrated in more than just Popeye cartoons.

Vegetable Potpies with Mashed Potato Crust

2 tablespoons olive oil

4 Yukon Gold potatoes, peeled
and diced

2 carrots, peeled and cut into
1-inch slices

1 onion, chopped

4 ounces green beans, cut into
1-inch pieces

2 stalks celery, chopped

1 cup green peas

5 mushrooms, sliced

1/4 cup flour

1 cup milk

2 cups vegetable broth

1/2 teaspoon each dried thyme,
dill, and tarragon

Salt and freshly ground pepper
to taste

Mashed Potato Crust

2 pounds baking (russet)
potatoes

2 tablespoons unsalted butter,
melted

1 egg, slightly beaten

2 tablespoons minced fresh
parsley

1 tablespoon minced fresh dill

Milk as needed

Serves 6

This is a good dish to make for kids, and one way to get them to eat their veggies. It's like shepherd's pie without the meat. Kids also like to help put the topping on the potpies; it's fun to sculpt the mashed potatoes. These potpies are definitely a comfort food.

Preheat the oven to 350°. In a large, heavy saucepan over medium heat, heat the olive oil and sauté the Yukon Gold potatoes, carrots, onion, green beans, celery, green peas, and mushrooms for 5 minutes.

In a small bowl, whisk the flour into the milk. Stir into a medium saucepan with the broth. Add the herbs and seasonings and bring to a boil. Reduce the heat to low and simmer, whisking frequently, until thickened, about 10 minutes. Gently stir this mixture into the sautéed vegetables. Spoon the vegetable mixture into individual crocks or casseroles.

Cook the baking potatoes in salted boiling water until tender, about 20 minutes. Drain and let cool to the touch. Peel and mash. Stir in half the butter, the egg, parsley, and dill until well blended. Add milk as necessary to achieve a smooth consistency. Top each crock or casserole with the mashed potatoes. Spread evenly to cover the surface. Use a fork to make peaks. Sprinkle with the remaining melted butter. Bake for 15 to 20 minutes, or until golden.

IN THE ENGLISH COURT OF HENRY VIII during the early 1500s, the nobility thought of vegetables as poor folks' food. According to one food historian, even their doctors believed that anything growing in the ground was dirty and contaminated and possibly even linked to diseases like the plague. As a result, almost all meals in the English court were centered around meats, game, and fowl, with a few carbohydrates thrown in.

Vegetable Potpies with Mashed Potato Crust

Desserts and Beverages

Applesauce Cake

1/2 cup unsalted butter at room
    temperature
1 cup sugar
1 egg
2 cups all-purpose flour
1 teaspoon baking powder
1 teaspoon baking soda
1/2 teaspoon ground allspice
    Pinch of salt
1 1/2 cups applesauce
3/4 cup walnuts, coarsely chopped

Makes one 9 x 5-inch loaf cake

This is a good cake to keep on hand at home, and it can also travel any and everywhere—in a lunch box, on the train, or on a Greyhound bus. I like it because it is easy to make, needs no frosting, and tastes soooo good—especially with a glass of Old-Fashioned Lemonade (page 147).

Preheat the oven to 350°. Grease and lightly flour a 9 x 5-inch loaf pan.

In a bowl, cream the butter and sugar together until light and fluffy. Add the egg and beat until smooth. In another bowl, stir the flour, baking powder, baking soda, allspice, and salt together. Alternately add the dry ingredients and applesauce to the mixture in thirds. Fold in the nuts. Spread the batter evenly in the pan and bake until a skewer inserted in the center comes out clean. Transfer the pan to a wire rack and let the cake cool completely. Cut into slices to serve.

EACH VARIETY OF APPLE HAS A UNIQUE flavor. Experiment with tastes. I know some people are real picky about what apple to do what with, but when making applesauce, the most important thing is a great-tasting apple. So experiment— you can mix Baldwins with McIntoshes or Cortlands with Rome Beauties.

Like apples, applesauce is versatile. It can be a side dish with meats, a topper for pancakes, or an ingredient in cakes and cookies. It can be spiked up with spices or with other fruits. It can be a comfort food by itself or a simple dessert with a dollop of whipped cream.

Bread Pudding

5 slices day-old bread, or
½ day-old baguette, sliced

2 eggs

3 tablespoons brown sugar

2 tablespoons granulated sugar,
plus more for sprinkling

¾ cup light cream or
half-and-half

1 teaspoon vanilla extract
Pinch of salt

½ teaspoon ground cinnamon

½ teaspoon ground nutmeg

½ cup raisins

3 tablespoons unsalted butter,
melted

Makes 4 to 6

Bread pudding came about when someone tried to think of a way to use up stale bread. This dish is pretty simple, but there are lots of variations. Some people add mixed fruit to their bread pudding. Some people put raisins in it, and some people put in nuts. Here's my recipe for a time-honored dessert.

Preheat the oven to 350°. Cut the bread into cubes and place in a buttered 8-inch square baking dish. In a bowl, whisk the eggs with the brown sugar and 1 tablespoon granulated sugar. Whisk in the cream or half-and-half and vanilla until blended. Pour this mixture over the bread and push the bread down into it.

In a small bowl, combine the salt, cinnamon, nutmeg, raisins, and the remaining 1 tablespoon sugar and mix together. Sprinkle this over the bread pudding. Pour the melted butter over the top. Sprinkle with granulated sugar to taste. Place the dish in a larger baking dish and add hot water to come halfway up the sides of the bread pudding dish. Bake for about 35 minutes, or until browned and set. Serve warm or at room temperature.

Corn Pudding

3¹/2 cups milk
   1 cup golden raisins
   1 cup yellow cornmeal
¹/2 cup dark molasses
      Pinch of salt
¹/2 cup sugar
   2 teaspoons ground ginger
¹/2 teaspoon freshly grated
      nutmeg
   2 tablespoons unsalted butter,
      melted
1¹/2 cups fresh or frozen corn
      kernels

Serves 8 to 10

Native American cooking still follows the ancient tradition of mixing various foods together for seasoning and tradition. Fruit and berries are used to add flavor to meat and fish. Vegetables, grains, and roots are combined into delicious stews. And, among all the native cultures of the Americas, the primary food is corn. Corn is sacred. It is the mother. There are songs, dances, stories, and ceremonies created around corn, or maize, its original name. Prayers are made to the corn spirits. It's prepared and eaten in a hundred different ways: on the cob, fried, and in stews, soups, and salads. It's cornmeal. It's hominy. And it comes in many colors: blue, red, yellow, white, and black. Here, it's used to make a dessert sometimes known as Indian pudding. This one has both corn kernels and cornmeal.

Preheat the oven to 300°. Butter a 2-quart casserole. In a large saucepan, heat 2 cups of the milk over medium-low heat until bubbles form around the edges. Stir in the raisins and set aside.

Place the cornmeal in a bowl and stir in the remaining 1¹/2 cups cold milk. Stir this mixture into the hot milk. Place the pan over medium-low heat and cook, stirring frequently, until the mixture thickens, 10 to 15 minutes. Stir in the molasses, salt, sugar, ginger, nutmeg, and butter until it is the consistency of hot cereal. Fold in the corn kernels.

Pour into the prepared casserole. Place the casserole in a baking pan and add warm water to a depth of about 2 inches. Bake for 1¹/2 to 2 hours, or until firm and browned. Let cool slightly before serving.

THOUSANDS OF AFRICAN SLAVES ESCAPED to Florida swamps, where they joined up with the Seminoles, Native Americans who had fled persecution and enforced relocation from the Southeast. In the eighteenth century, it is estimated that there were over 100,000 black Indians resulting from the mixture of these peoples. Today, most black Seminoles live along the Rio Grande in the United States and across the border in northern Mexico.

Pineapple Upside-Down Cake

7 tablespoons unsalted butter at
   room temperature
1/4 cup packed brown sugar
7 canned pineapple rings,
   drained
7 maraschino cherries, drained
1 1/4 cups cake flour
1 1/2 teaspoons baking powder
1/4 teaspoon salt
3/4 cup granulated sugar
2 eggs
1/2 cup milk
2 tablespoons Myers's rum
1 teaspoon vanilla extract

Makes one 12-inch cake

When European explorers arrived on this side of the Atlantic, they discovered a wealth of delicious fruits unlike anything they had tasted before. Columbus made his second voyage in 1493, and one of his landing parties got lost in a rain forest on the island of Guadeloupe. When his sailors emerged 5 days later, they were carrying new golden treasures: pineapples. This is a recipe for a cake made from one of these treasures. If you want to use fresh pineapple in this recipe, heat the slices first in a light syrup made with 1 cup sugar and 2 cups water.

Preheat the oven to 350°. In a 12-inch ovenproof skillet, melt 3 table-spoons of the butter over low heat. Brush the sides of the pan with the butter and sprinkle the brown sugar over the bottom of the pan. Arrange the pineapple slices in the pan and put a cherry in the center of each slice. Set aside.

In a bowl, stir the flour, baking powder, and salt together. In another bowl, beat the remaining 4 tablespoons butter until creamy. Beat in the granulated sugar until smooth. Beat in the eggs one at a time. Alternately stir in the flour mixture and milk in thirds, stirring until smooth after each addition. Fold in the rum and vanilla. Spread the batter over the fruit. Bake for 30 minutes, or until a skewer inserted in the center comes out clean. Let stand for 5 minutes before invert-ing to unmold on a serving plate.

YOU KNOW, PEOPLE OFTEN ASSOCIATE the pineapple with Hawaii, but no one really knows when the pineapple arrived there. There was no record of it in 1778, when Captain Cook's botanist recorded the plants of the island. Hawaiians called the pineapple halakahiki. *Hala refers to a native Hawaiian plant that sort of looks like a pineapple, and* kahiki *is Hawaiian for "foreign" or "foreign land." So* halakahiki *means "a plant from a foreign land."*

The Indians on the Caribbean islands had enjoyed pineapples for centuries before the Spanish came. They called them na-na, *which meant "fragrance" or "excellent fruit." The Spanish called them* piñas *or* ananas. *In the court of King Ferdinand, they just called them delicious—the best of the tropical fruits.*

Black Cake

3 cups (1¹/2 pounds) mixed dried
    fruits such as chopped
    dates, raisins, dried cur-
    rants, and prunes
1 cup port or sweet wine, plus
    more as needed
1 cup Myers's rum, plus more as
    needed
1 cup unsalted butter at room
    temperature
1¹/2 cups packed dark brown sugar
3 eggs
1¹/2 pounds garnet yams, peeled
    and grated
1 cup all-purpose flour
    Dash of salt
1 tablespoon baking powder
1 teaspoon ground cinnamon
1 teaspoon ground ginger
¹/2 teaspoon freshly grated
    nutmeg
¹/2 teaspoon ground mace
¹/2 teaspoon ground allspice

The Caribbean has many versions of this fruitcake, which is the traditional English Christmas cake transformed into a dark, tropical
delight. It's not like those hard, dry fruitcakes some people try to
foist off on you at Christmas! This Jamaican version is almost black,
and moist with dark dried fruits, brown sugar, and yams. It's a recipe
from Heidi Haughy Cusick's *Soul and Spice,* but with a traditional
Christmas icing and decoration added. This kind of cake is very
popular at African-American weddings.

At least 1 month before cooking, place the fruit in a large bowl or
wide-mouthed jar and add wine and rum to cover the fruit. Cover and
store in a dark place, stirring occasionally and adding more wine or
rum as needed to completely cover the fruit.

When ready to bake, generously butter a 4-quart Bundt or tube pan.
Preheat the oven to 300°.

In a large bowl, beat the butter and sugar together until light and
fluffy. Beat in the eggs, one at a time. Add the yams and mix well.
In a medium bowl, stir the flour, salt, baking powder, and spices
together. Stir into the yam mixture.

Icing and Decoration

1 1/2 cups powdered sugar, sifted

2 tablespoons milk or cream

1 to 3 teaspoons freshly
squeezed lemon juice
Candied cherries, nuts,
and/or candied citrus peel,
for decorating

Makes 1 cake; serves 10 to 12

Drain the soaked fruit, reserving the soaking liquid. In a blender or food processor, process the fruit and a little of the reserved liquid to make a coarse purée. Add the purée to the yam mixture. Stir in 1/2 cup of the reserved soaking liquid. Pour the batter into the prepared pan.

Cover the pan tightly with aluminum foil and bake for about 1 hour, or until risen and set. Remove from the oven, uncover, and let cool to room temperature, about 1 hour. Loosen the sides of the cake with a thin knife, place a serving plate over the top of the pan, and invert. Lift off the pan. Decorate the cake now, or store for later. To store, spread a little of the remaining reserved soaking liquid over the top of the cake, cover the cake, and refrigerate for up to 1 week.

To serve, bring the cake to room temperature if necessary. To decorate the cake: Place the powdered sugar in a bowl and stir in the milk or cream. Add lemon juice as necessary to make a thick icing. Spoon and spread the icing over the top of the cake, letting it drip down the sides. Decorate the top of the cake with candied cherries, nuts, and/or candied citrus peel.

Tres Leches

(Three-Milk Cake)

1 cup sugar
5 eggs, separated
1/3 cup milk
1/2 teaspoon vanilla extract
1 cup all-purpose flour
1 1/2 teaspoons baking powder
Pinch of salt
1/4 teaspoon cream of tartar

Milk Syrup

1 3/4 cups evaporated milk
1 cup sweetened condensed milk
1 cup heavy cream
1 teaspoon vanilla extract
1 tablespoon dark rum

Topping

1 1/2 cups heavy cream
1 teaspoon vanilla extract
1/4 cup sugar

Makes one 12 x 9-inch cake;
serves 12

I'm not quite sure where this cake is from, but Nicaraguans, Cubans, and Costa Ricans all claim it. All I know is that it's eaten all over the Americas and it's delicious. The three different milks are condensed milk, evaporated milk, and regular milk, and heavy cream is in there too. Canned milks are used in many Latin American recipes because of the lack of refrigeration in some areas.

Preheat the oven to 350°. Grease a 12 x 9-inch glass baking dish. In a large bowl, beat 3/4 cup of the sugar with the egg yolks until light and fluffy. Whisk in the milk and vanilla. In a small bowl, stir the flour, baking powder, and salt together. Gradually whisk the dry ingredients into the wet ingredients.

In a large bowl, beat the egg whites until foamy. Add the cream of tartar and beat until soft peaks form. Gradually beat in the remaining 1/4 cup sugar and continue beating until stiff, glossy peaks form. Stir one fourth of the whites into the yolk mixture, then gently fold in the remaining whites until blended. Spoon the batter into the prepared dish.

Bake the cake for 20 minutes, or until a toothpick inserted in the center comes out clean. Let the cake cool completely in the dish.

To make the milk syrup: In a bowl, stir all the ingredients together until thoroughly mixed. Pierce the cake all over with a fork. Pour the syrup over the top of the cake.

To make the topping: In a large, deep bowl, beat the cream until soft peaks form. Beat in the vanilla until blended, then beat in the sugar until stiff peaks form. Spread the topping over the cake.

Refrigerate for 2 hours before cutting into squares to serve.

Camote

3 sweet potatoes or yams

1/2 pineapple, peeled, cored, and chopped

1 1/2 cups granulated sugar

1/2 cup packed brown sugar

1/2 tablespoon ground cinnamon
Coconut flakes, for sprinkling

Serves 4 to 6

Sometimes I just have to have something sweet. I know someone who always wants to know what's for dessert before she picks a meal, and will go so far as to check out the dessert side of a restaurant's menu before deciding to eat there. This is an outstanding and unusual Mexican dessert made with sweet potatoes, from my friend chef Dudley Nieto. I can also imagine serving this as a side dish with roast turkey, pork, or ham.

In a large pot, cook the sweet potatoes in simmering water to cover for about 20 minutes, or until tender when pierced with a knife. Let cool to the touch and peel.

In a large, heavy pot, combine the sweet potatoes and pineapple. Stir in the sugars and simmer over low heat, stirring occasionally, for 30 to 45 minutes. Stir in the cinnamon. Serve in glass bowls with the coconut sprinkled over.

Island Fruit Supreme

1 mango, peeled, cut from the
   pit, and diced
1 small papaya, peeled, seeded,
   and diced
1/2 fresh pineapple, peeled, cored,
   and diced
2 small bananas, peeled and
   sliced
1/4 cup Myers's rum
2 tablespoons freshly squeezed
   lime juice, or to taste
2 tablespoons sugar, or to taste
1/4 cup unsweetened grated
   coconut

Serves 6

The coconut is a versatile fruit. Over the years, just about every part of the coconut palm and its fruit has been used—even to build houses and rafts, and to make rope from the husk fibers. There's coconut meat and there's coconut water, both popular treats in the West Indies. And, of course, coconut oil is still a popular cooking oil with Caribbean chefs. One of the best uses for coconut meat is in desserts, like this dessert fruit salad.

In a large bowl, combine all the ingredients except the coconut and gently blend. Cover and refrigerate for at least 2 hours. Fold in the coconut just before serving.

CHRISTOPHER COLUMBUS MAY HAVE founded the rum industry by bringing sugarcane to the Caribbean in 1493, but the Puritans helped to make this drink popular in the States. Its manufacture was so profitable that in 1750 there were sixty-three distilleries in Massachusetts.

Lime Meringue Pie

2 tablespoons flour
4 tablespoons cornstarch
3 tablespoons cold water
2 tablespoons grated lime zest
  Juice of 6 limes
1 cup granulated sugar
3 eggs, separated
  Pinch of salt
3/4 cup superfine sugar
1 baked 8-inch pie crust

Makes one 8-inch pie

Nothing is better than homemade lemon meringue pie, unless it's lime meringue pie. It won't be bright green, just a pale greenish yellow. But this is the perfect dessert to serve with Caribbean food or after a pork or fish dinner. Your guests will thank you.

In a saucepan, mix the flour and cornstarch together. Add the water and stir to make a smooth paste. Stir in the lime zest, juice, and granulated sugar. Bring to a boil over medium heat, stirring constantly. Cook at a rapid boil for 2 minutes, stirring. Remove from the heat and let cool to lukewarm. Beat the egg yolks into the mixture and bring to a simmer over low heat; do not boil. Cook, stirring, for 3 minutes. Remove from the heat and pour into the pie crust. Let cool completely.

To make the meringue, preheat the oven to 425°. In a large bowl, beat the egg whites with the salt until soft peaks form. Gradually beat in the superfine sugar until stiff, glossy peaks form. Spread the meringue over the top of the pie all the way to the crust. Make peaks in the meringue with a spoon. Bake in the center of the oven for 10 to 15 minutes, or until the meringue is lightly browned. Let cool completely before serving.

LIMES, LIKE COCONUT, RUM, AND Scotch bonnet chilies, are one of the most important Caribbean flavors. You can use lime juice to marinate foods, to make refreshing drinks, and to make desserts for Caribbean dinners. Use it like lemon juice to add a spark to all kinds of dishes; like salt, these citrus juices bring out the flavors of foods. One of the simplest ways to use limes is to serve wedges of them along with sliced tropical fruits such as mangos and papayas. A squeeze of lime adds a lively taste to the sweet-sweet fruit. It's good on melons, too.

Milk Custard

3/4 cup sugar

4 eggs

1 (7-ounce) can sweetened
   condensed milk

1 (8-ounce) can evaporated milk

7/8 cup water

1 teaspoon vanilla extract

Serves 6

Variations of this caramelized custard are served all through Latin countries. The mother dessert was the flan from Spain, which is now beloved in Mexico. This is a Cuban version.

Preheat the oven to 350°. Place the sugar in a small, heavy skillet over medium-low heat. Stir until melted and caramelized to a medium brown. Pour the caramel into a 6-cup glass, ceramic, or metal mold, or into a 10-inch glass pie plate. Rotate the mold or plate to evenly coat the bottom and sides with the caramel.

In a large bowl, beat the eggs. Whisk in the milks, water, and vanilla. Strain through a fine-meshed sieve. Pour into the mold. Place the mold in a baking pan and add hot water to come halfway up the side of the mold. Bake for about 1 hour, or until the custard is firm and a knife inserted halfway into the center comes out clean. Let cool completely. Refrigerate for at least 2 hours. Unmold by placing a plate on top of the mold or pie plate; invert and remove the mold or plate.

NOTHING HAS BEEN MORE IMPORTANT to Cuba than sugar. At the time of Columbus's voyages, sugar was so precious in Europe that it was sold by the tablespoon. The Caribbean climate was perfect for growing sugarcane. Sugar became the gold that the Spanish had come looking for. In 1791, after the slave revolt in Haiti, Cuba became the leading sugar producer in the Caribbean. In fact, a leading Cuba landowner once said, "Without sugar, there is no Cuba."

Peach Cobbler

6 ripe peaches

1/2 cup sugar

2 teaspoons tapioca

1/2 teaspoon vanilla extract

4 tablespoons unsalted butter, melted

Topping

11/2 cups all-purpose flour

3 tablespoons sugar

2 teaspoons baking powder

1/2 teaspoon baking soda

1/4 teaspoon salt

1/2 cup buttermilk

1 egg

Serves 4 to 5

A friend of mine told me his grandmother made the best peach cobbler ever—it was so juicy. But when his wife made it, the cobbler was missing the juice. Well, for cobbler you have to use juicy peaches. It's best to just make cobbler in the summer when peaches are really ripe and flavorful. If you have to have cobbler another time, use defrosted frozen sliced peaches.

Preheat the oven to 400°. Drop the peaches in a large saucepan of boiling water for about 10 seconds. Using a slotted spoon, transfer them to a bowl of cold water to cool. Drain, peel, pit, and cut into slices. Place in a large bowl and add the sugar, tapioca, and vanilla. Mix well and pour into an 8-inch square baking dish. Drizzle with the butter.

To make the topping: In a bowl, stir all the dry ingredients together. In another bowl, whisk the buttermilk and egg together until blended. Stir the buttermilk mixture into the dry ingredients just until blended; the batter will be lumpy. Spoon the dough over the peaches in a cobblestone effect. (I guess that's why they call it cobbler. But some people say it's because it's cobbled together.) Bake until the topping is golden brown, 20 to 25 minutes. Let cool slightly. Serve warm.

Shoofly Pie

1 unbaked 8-inch pie crust

3/4 cup all-purpose flour

1/4 cup sugar

Pinch of salt

1/2 teaspoon baking soda

1/4 teaspoon freshly grated nutmeg

1/4 teaspoon ground ginger

1/4 teaspoon ground cloves

1/4 teaspoon ground cinnamon

3 tablespoons cold unsalted butter, cut into bits

1 egg, lightly beaten

1/2 cup dark molasses

Whipped cream, for serving

Makes one 8-inch pie

During the eighteenth century, the Caribbean Islands produced 80 to 90 percent of the sugar consumed by Western Europeans. This demand made quite a living for the plantation owners, who became the very definition of wealth. "Rich as a West Indian planter" was a common reference to their lavish lifestyle.

The growing availability of sugar gave people a sweet tooth, so they used more sugar, as well as any sugar by-product they could get their hands on. This recipe uses a sugar by-product, molasses. Down South, we call this dessert molasses pie or spice pie, but the Pennsylvania Dutch call it shoofly pie.

Preheat the oven to 400°. Prick the pie crust all over with a fork. Fit a square of aluminum foil into the pie crust and fill it with dried beans or pie weights. Partially bake the pie crust for 5 to 10 minutes, or until just set. Remove the foil and beans or weights. Reduce the oven temperature to 350°.

In a bowl, stir the flour, sugar, salt, baking soda, and spices together. Add the butter and work into the flour mixture with your fingers or a pastry cutter until the mixture looks like crumbs. In another bowl, mix the egg and molasses together. Add the crumb mixture and stir until blended. Pour the filling into the crust and bake until set, 35 to 40 minutes. Let cool to room temperature before cutting into wedges. Serve each slice with a dollop of whipped cream.

MOLASSES IS A RESULT OF THE REFINING of sugarcane and sugar beets. The juice squeezed from these plants is boiled to a syrupy mixture. Sugar crystals are taken from the mixture, and the remaining brown liquid is molasses. Some folks swear by the health benefits of molasses, particularly blackstrap molasses, the strongest kind. It's supposed to be really good for you because it's high in calcium, iron, and other minerals. But I just like the way molasses tastes.

Coquito

2 cups Myers's rum
2 (12-ounce) cans evaporated
    milk
1 (15-ounce) can coconut cream
    Sugar to taste
1 teaspoon ground cinnamon
1 tablespoon vanilla extract

Makes about 6 cups; serves 12

This drink from Puerto Rico is so rich and potent that, like eggnog, a little goes a long way. In fact, it's a nice change from eggnog. You could serve it at a tropical Christmas party, with Black Cake (page 134).

In a punch bowl, combine all the ingredients and mix until blended. Serve over crushed ice.

Jamaica Water

2 cups dried jamaica flowers
    (available in Latino markets)
2 tablespoons grated fresh
    ginger
1 teaspoon grated orange zest
4 cups boiling water
    Sugar to taste
8 cups cold water, or to taste

Makes about 3 quarts

This beautiful red drink, which looks almost like cranberry juice, is made from dried hibiscus flowers. It's popular throughout the Caribbean and Mexico, where you often see giant glass jars of it in the markets. Jamaica flowers may also be labelled *rosella, roselle,* or sorrel, although they are completely different from the green vegetable also known as sorrel.

Place the jamaica flowers in a large pot and add the ginger and orange zest. Add the boiling water and let steep overnight. Strain the mixture. Add the sugar and mix well. Pour into a sterilized quart jar and let the mixture sit for 2 days. To serve, mix with the cold water. Taste and adjust the sweetening. Serve over ice.

Old-Fashioned Lemonade

1 cup sugar
5 cups water
2 lemon peels, sliced
   Juice from 8 lemons

Makes about 6 cups

This takes a little more time than frozen lemonade, but the taste will conjure up memories of the days when the only lemonade was real lemonade, made from real lemons. Now, I can drink iced tea all year round, but to me, lemonade means summer.

In a saucepan, combine the sugar, 2 cups of the water, and the lemon peels. Bring to a simmer and cook for 10 minutes. Let cool and strain into a pitcher. Add the lemon juice and the remaining 3 cups water. Stir and chill. Serve over ice.

Orangey Minted Tea

1 lemon
2 oranges
3 tablespoons loose black tea
   Fresh mint leaves
4 cups boiling water
1 cup sugar

Makes about 5 cups

I always know I'm in the South when the waitress asks me if I want my iced tea sweetened or unsweetened. Southerners know that you just can't get sugar to dissolve in cold iced tea. Most people there drink it with sugar, and when you go to their homes, they'll bring out a pitcher of sweetened iced tea.

Squeeze the juice from the lemon and oranges. Cut the lemon and orange peel into strips. Place in a bowl with the tea and mint. Pour the boiling water over. Add the sugar and stir. Let steep until cool. Add the lemon and orange juice. Stir and chill. Serve over ice.

Atole

4 cups water

1 tablet Mexican chocolate

1/2 tablespoon packed brown
sugar, or more to taste

8 ounces prepared fresh corn
masa, or 1 cup masa harina,
dissolved in 1 cup hot water

Serves 4 to 6

The great emperor Montezuma loved chocolate. His dinners were
not complete without his beloved *atole,* a prehistoric corn and
chocolate beverage. It is said that he drank as many as fifty cups
of *atole* every day. Here's a recipe for this traditional drink, adapted
from one given to me by chef Dudley Nieto.

In a saucepan, bring the water to a simmer. Add the chocolate
and stir until dissolved. Stir in the sugar, then gradually stir in the
dissolved masa or masa harina. Beat with a whisk until frothy.
Serve hot.

*THE COCOA BEAN WAS THOUGHT TO BE
a gift from the gods from the days of
the Mayans and was so prized that it
was often used as a form of currency.*

*For instance, a bean might be traded for
a small tomato, and ten beans could
buy you a rabbit. Cocoa was that important to the Mayan and Aztec peoples.*

Mango Fool

4 mangos, peeled, cut from the pits, and chopped
3 tablespoons freshly squeezed lime juice
3 tablespoons Myers's rum
1/4 teaspoon ground cinnamon
1/2 cup superfine sugar
1 cup heavy cream, whipped to stiff peaks and chilled

Makes 6

Do you know a fool? They're delicious. A "fool" is a chilled fruit purée that is folded into whipped cream. It is smooth and wonderful. Any fruit can be used, but mango gives this fluffy dessert its distinctive Caribbean accent.

In a blender or food processor, combine the chopped mangos, lime juice, and rum and purée until smooth. Add the cinnamon and sugar and purée until blended. Pour into a bowl. Cover and refrigerate for at least 2 hours or up to 24 hours. Just before serving, fold in the whipped cream. Serve in one large bowl or individual bowls or glasses.

MANGOS, NATIVE TO SOUTHEASTERN Asia, have been growing for over four thousand years. In the sixteenth century, they made their way to Africa. By the early seventeenth century, they were in Brazil, and by the century's end, mangos were found growing all over the West Indies. According to one story, *these fragrant little ovals might just have floated from ships to the shores of the Caribbean Islands, where they have been a staple ever since. Both green and ripe mangos are used in sauces, chutneys, and salsas. Ripe mangos are used in candies and drinks, or enjoyed just as they are.*

Ingredient Glossary

Ackee: A red, pear-shaped fruit with a yellow flesh. Originally from Africa, it is now grown in Jamaica and used in many dishes, especially with cod-fish. It is available canned in some West Indian markets.

Callalou: The greens of the taro root, used to make a popular Caribbean dish. Collard greens, kale, or spinach may be substituted.

Canola oil: A mild-tasting, health-ful oil made from rapeseed, this oil is lower in saturated fat than any other.

Cassava: *See* Yuca.

Cassava meal: *See* Manioc flour.

Chayote: A pale green fruit about the size of a mango, with a furrowed skin. It is quite bland and is good in dishes with assertive seasonings. The chayote is popular throughout the Caribbean, Deep South, Mexico, and Central America. Look for it in Latino and West Indian markets and some supermarkets. It is also known as *christophene* and mirliton.

Chipotle chilies: Dried smoked jalapeño chilies, these are available dried or canned in adobo, a spicy sauce. The canned ones are easier to use for most dishes.

Chorizo sausage: Originally from Spain, this sausage is also made in Mexico. Use Mexican chorizo when it is called for in a recipe, as this ver-sion uses fresh pork; Spanish chorizo used smoked pork and will give a dish a slightly different taste.

Coconut cream: A more concen-trated version of coconut milk, this is made using less water and so is thicker and richer. Don't confuse it with cream of coconut, which is sweetened.

Coconut milk: Made by simmering fresh or dried coconut in water, coconut milk adds an inimitable taste and texture to foods. Available in cans in West Indian and Asian markets.

Conch: A shellfish used in Asian and West Indian cooking, it is sold fresh, in its shell, or frozen. In any case, like abalone, it must be pounded until thin and then shredded in order to tenderize the meat. Look for it frozen in West Indian markets.

Djon djon mushrooms: A mush-room that grows wild in Haiti and is used dried to make a popular rice Haitian dish, *riz djon djon*. It may be found in West Indian markets, but dried shiitakes are an excellent sub-stitute.

Epazote: A pungent green that grows wild throughout the United States and Mexico. Used in Mexican cooking, especially in bean dishes and soups, it is sometimes available fresh in Latino markets. There is no real substitute, but cilantro may be used in place of it.

Grouper: A kind of sea bass. There are several varieties, found on both the Atlantic and Pacific coasts. Grouper is a mainstay of Bahamian cuisine. Any firm, white-fleshed fish may be substituted.

Güero chilies: A pale yellow, piquant fresh chili used in Mexican cuisine. It is available in Latino mar-kets. The elongated yellow Italian chilies may be substituted.

Habanero chilies: Very closely related to the Scotch bonnet chili and similar in appearance, these round, knobby, yellow chilies may be substi-tuted for the Scotch bonnet.

Jalapeño chilies: Available green or red, jalapeños are about 2 inches long, shiny, and very hot. Serrano chilies may be substituted. Wash your hands in hot, soapy water after handling these. They are also avail-able pickled, but should be used fresh unless the recipe specifies pickled jalapeños.

Jamaica flowers: Dried hibiscus flowers, used to make a dark red tea or cold drink in Caribbean countries and Mexico. Confusingly, they are also known as sorrel in the West Indies.

Jerk sauce: A prepared sauce with a base of jerk seasoning; available in West Indian markets and specialty foods store.

Jerk seasoning: A mix of dried piquant spices used in Jamaican cooking. Available in West Indian markets and specialty foods stores.

Kielbasa: A garlicky Polish sausage.

Linguiça: A garlicky Portuguese sausage.

Manioc flour: A starchy substance derived from yuca, or cassava root. It is also known as cassava meal. Look for it in West Indian markets, or look for it under its other name, tapioca flour, in supermarkets.

Masa: Prepared fresh corn masa is used to make tortillas and tamales. It is a ground paste made from wet corn that has been soaked in lime water. Fresh masa is available from some Latino groceries and restaurants.

Masa harina: A flour made from dried fresh masa. It is also used to make tortillas, with water added. It is available in sacks in Latino markets.

Mexican chocolate: Pressed tablets of chocolate that have been ground with almonds and vanilla. Available in Latino markets.

Mexican oregano: A strongly flavored variety of oregano, used dried in Mexican cooking. It is available in Latino markets, but regular dried oregano may be substituted.

Myers's rum: A dark, flavorful rum from Jamaica.

Nopal: The paddle of the prickly pear cactus, the nopal must be cleaned of its bumps and spines, then cooked before using. It is a popular ingredient in Mexican dishes, especially salads.

Nopalitos: Julienne-cut nopal cactus; *see* Nopal.

Okra: A green vegetable pod, originally from Africa and used in Southern foods such as gumbo. It is available fresh or frozen.

Panela cheese: A mild, somewhat salty Indian cheese often used as a substitute for queso fresco.

Pepitas: *See* Pumpkin seeds.

Pigeon peas: Also called Congo peas or *gungo* peas, these peas, originally from Africa, are pale yellow, with an "eye," like black-eyed peas. Black-eyed peas may be substituted.

Piri-piri sauce: *Piri-piri* is an African word for hot pepper; the name is used to refer to any hot pepper sauce, such as Tabasco.

Plantains: Related to the banana, but starchier, the plantain must be cooked before eating. Green plantains are firmer and preferred for frying, but yellow ones with black spots will work well also. Fully ripe plantains are almost black on the outside.

Poblano chilies: Black-green triangular-shaped fresh chilies, about 4 inches long, these have a deep, smoky taste. There is no real substitute for the unique taste of poblanos, so look for them in Latino markets and specialty foods stores.

Polenta: Coarsely ground cornmeal. A staple of Italian cooking, it is cooked into a thick mush, like cornmeal mush, and is also sometimes fried.

Pumpkin seeds: Hulled pumpkin seeds are available in Latino markets, where they may be called *pepitas*. Ground pumpkin seeds are used to make *pipián*, a seed-based mole.

Queso fresco: A mild, fresh white Mexican cheese that crumbles easily. Panela cheese or feta cheese may be substituted.

Saffron: The stigmas of a Mediterranean crocus, saffron is available in thread form (the dried stigmas) or ground. It adds a brilliant golden color and a slightly acidic taste to foods.

Salt cod: Dried, salted codfish, used in many coastal cuisines, such as Mediterranean, Caribbean, and that of the Atlantic coast. The flat, hard white fish needs to be soaked and drained before using, and salt cod with bones must be boned. Also called saltfish or dried cod.

Saltfish: *See* Salt cod.

Scotch bonnet chilies: These chilies do look like the tam-o'-shanters worn by Scotsmen in kilts, but they are golden yellow. One of the hottest of all chilies, they should be handled and used with care. Use less to start with than you think you'll want, and increase to taste in very small quantities. Wash your hands with hot soapy water after handling them. Habanero chilies are almost identical and may be substituted. If you can't find either fresh chili, use cayenne pepper to taste instead.

Serrano chilies: Slightly larger than jalapeños, but similar in shape, these elongated shiny fresh chilies are available either green or red. They may be interchanged with fresh jalapeños.

Tapioca flour: *See* Manioc flour.

Tomatillos: These look like small green tomatoes with a papery husk, but they are really a kind of ground cherry. They have a lemony, mild taste and are used in Mexican cooking. The husk must be removed before using. Tomatillos are available fresh in Latino markets, but canned ones may be used for salsas and soups.

Yuca: A large starchy tuber native to Brazil. It has a white bland-tasting flesh and is cooked and eaten like the potato. Yuca is also known as cassava and is the source of manioc flour, also known as tapioca flour or cassava meal.

Mail Order Sources

Here is a partial list of mail order sources for the foodstuffs used in this book, as well as sources for Southern/Creole foods. Many have catalogs available upon request that offer a wide range of products.

A & W Island Food Store
2634 San Pablo Avenue
Berkeley, CA 94702
510-649-9195
(African yams, plantains, salted mackerel, pigeon peas, Caribbean spices)

Adams Milling Company
Route 6, Box 148A
Dothan, AL 36303
800-239-4233
(Grits milled from whole kernel corn and other corn products, such as water-ground cornmeal)

Basse's Choice
P.O. Box 1
Smithfield, VA 23431
800-292-2773
(Smithfield hams, Williamsburg slab bacon)

Battistella's Seafood, Inc.
910 Touro Street
New Orleans, LA 70116
504-949-2724
(Live crawfish, catfish, crab products)

Bueno Foods
Mail Order Department
2001 Fourth Street SW
Albuquerque, NM 87102
800-95CHILE
web site: www.buenofoods.com
(Chile sauces, various spices, cornmeal, *posole*, cookbooks)

The Company Store
1039 Decatur Street
New Orleans, LA 70116
800-772-2927
(Café du Monde coffee, beignet mix, spices, cookbooks)

DeKalb World Farmer's Market
3000 East Ponce de Leon Avenue
Decatur, GA 30030
404-377-6401
(Fresh seasonal produce, Caribbean seasonings, dried shrimp)

Hoppin' John's
30 Pinckney Street
Charleston, SC 29401
843-577-6404
(Stone-ground cornmeal, corn flour)

Konriko Company Store
307 Ann Street
New Iberia, LA 70562
800-551-3245
(Louisiana rice, Creole seasonings, bases for gumbo, crawfish boil)

La Caja China
7822 Northwest 72nd Avenue
Miami, FL 33166
800-338-1323
(China boxes; see page 96 for description. When ordering, ask for "Model #1")

Mo Hotta Mo Betta
P.O. Box 4136
San Luis Obispo, CA 93403
800-462-3220
web site: www.mohotta.com
(Hot sauces and spices from around the world, Mo Hotta clothing, hot sauce cookbooks)

SalsaMex
P.O. Box 1128
Mount Pleasant, SC 29464
888-725-7269
web site: www.salsamex.com
(Various salsas)

Sunnyland Farms, Inc.
P.O. Box 8200
Albany, GA 31706-8200
912-883-3085
(Pecans, fruits, candies)

Band G Foods
426 Eagle Rock Avenue
Roseland, NJ 07068
973-228-2500
(Hot sauces)

W.B. Roddenbery Co., Inc.
P.O. Box 60
Cairo, GA 31728
912-377-2102
(Boiled peanuts)

Index

WTTW Acknowledgments Production Credits

You can't make a great television show without a team of expert hard-working professionals who have a passionate commitment to making magic. A cooking show requires the collaboration of many diverse talents, from chefs and food stylists to the production staff, engineers, floor crew and designers. I am humbled by the hard work and love displayed by these talented individuals.

Thank you, Vertamae, for your brilliant creativity and passion. A special thanks to Dan Schmidt, WTTW President and CEO, and Mary Beth Hughes, Sr. Vice President for the Chicago Production Center, for embracing the project. And my deepest gratitude to Katherine Lauderdale, Sr. Vice President, New Ventures, and Ron Nigro, Director, New Ventures, for their continuing hard work and support of *The Americas' Family Kitchen*.

I extend my heartfelt thanks to the entire production team and to those individuals and companies who donated their time, talent, furnishings, and equipment in support of *The Americas' Family Kitchen* with Vertamae Grosvenor. It was a divine pleasure working with all of you.

Frances J. Harth
Executive Producer
Chicago 1998

Production Staff

Michael D. McAlpin	Producer
Tim Ward	Director
Kaye Benson	Writer/Researcher
Yevette Lewis Brown	Segment Producer
Cynthia Malek	Associate Director
Michael Loewenstein	Scenic Design
Cindy McCullough	Graphic Design
Julie Anderson	Production Assistant
Lydia Brauer	Production Assistant
Simon Carruthers, II	Production Assistant
April R. Davis	Production Assistant
Courtney E. Garland	Production Assistant
Preston Harris, II	Production Assistant
Aimee Tolson	Make-up
Shaunese Teamer	Publicist
Angela Revier	Production Intern
Vermille Seribo	Production Intern

Kitchen Staff

Sylvia Anderson	Kitchen Staff
Megan Dawson	Kitchen Staff
Jean McRae	Kitchen Staff
Larry Tucker	Chef
Dudley Nieto	Chef

Special Thanks To:

Casimiro González
Darlene Davis
Guadeloupe Garcia Vasquez
Hebert Bottex
Pamela Nunes
Alix LaFond
Guillermo Ohem
Martha Varela
Haitian Ministry of Tourism
El Rancho Hotel
Bahamas Ministry of Tourism
Radisson Hotel - Paradise Island
Fiesta Americana Hotel - Mexico City & Veracruz
Fiesta Inn Hotel - Xalapa
Mexican Government Tourism Office
Expo Mexico

Studio/Post Production Staff

Al Williams	Production Manager
Carlos Tronshaw	Camera
Ricky Wells	Camera
Emmett E. Wilson	Camera
Chuck Haynie	Camera
Derrick Young	Camera
Raymond O. Meinke	Camera
Roy D. Alan	Camera
Richard J. Well	Technical Director
Jim Gedwellas	Lighting Director
John Kennamer	Audio
William Alvelo	Field Audio
Marvin J. Pienta	Floor Director
Mark Anderson	Tape
Kim R. Breitenbach	Floor Assistant
Danny Rozkuszka	Floor Assistant
Maurice Smith	Floor Assistant
Steve Miller	Video
Barbara E. Allen	Off-line Editor
Paul Thornton	On-line Editor
Jerry Binder	On-line Audio
Robert Dove	On-line Audio
Jim Guthrie	On-line Audio
Barbara Shintani	Electronic Titles